D0854268

DUEL

Also by Richard Dunwoody

HELL FOR LEATHER: A CHAMPION'S DIARY
(WITH MARCUS ARMYTAGE)

Also by Sean Magee

THE CHANNEL FOUR BOOK OF RACING
THE CHANNEL FOUR BOOK OF THE RACING YEAR
GREAT RACES
THAT'S RACING (EDITED WITH PETER O'SULLEVAN)
RACING AND THE IRISH
RUNNERS AND RIDERS

DUEL
THE CHAMPION'S DEFENCE

RICHARD DUNWOODY
with SEAN MAGEE

PARTRIDGE PRESS

LONDON · NEW YORK · TORONTO · SYDNEY · AUCKLAND

TRANSWORLD PUBLISHERS LTD
61–63 Uxbridge Road, London W5 5SA

TRANSWORLD PUBLISHERS (AUSTRALIA) PTY LTD
15–25 Helles Avenue, Moorebank, NSW 2170

TRANSWORLD PUBLISHERS (NZ) LTD
3 William Pickering Drive, Albany, Auckland

Published 1994 by Partridge Press
a division of Transworld Publishers Ltd
Copyright © Richard Dunwoody and Sean Magee 1994

The right of Richard Dunwoody and Sean Magee to be identified as
authors of this work has been asserted in accordance with sections
77 and 78 of the Copyright Designs and Patents Act 1988.

The publishers have made every effort to trace the owners of
photographs used in this book. In any cases where they have been
unsuccessful they invite copyright holders to contact them direct.

A catalogue record for this book is available from
the British Library.

ISBN 185225 2367

This book is sold subject to the Standard Conditions of Sale of Net
Books and may not be resold in the UK below the net price fixed by
the publishers for the book.

All rights reserved. No part of this publications may be reproduced,
stored in a retrieval system, or transmitted in any form or by any
means, electronic, mechanical, photocopying, recording, or otherwise,
without the prior permission of the publishers.

Typeset in Sabon 11/15pt by
Hewer Text Composition Services, Edinburgh

Printed in Great Britain by Mackays of Chatham Plc, Chatham, Kent

CONTENTS

PREFACE

From Bangor-on-Dee, just over the Welsh border near Wrexham, to Market Rasen in deepest Lincolnshire, is about 110 miles as the crow flies.

During the 1993–4 National Hunt season Richard Dunwoody and Adrian Maguire made that journey by a rather more circuitous route than the average crow, taking over ten months and tens of thousands of miles by car, plane and helicopter, as they fought out the most memorable jump jockeys' championship in recent memory.

By the end of their journey at Market Rasen on a blustery evening on the first Saturday of June they were scarcely more divided in terms of winners ridden than they had been back at Bangor on the last Friday of the previous July. In the history of close contests, it was jump racing's answer to Michael Thomas's winning the 1989 League Championship for Arsenal with the last kick of the season against Liverpool, or Dennis Taylor beating Steve Davis on the final black in the 1985 World Snooker Championships.

This book tells the story of their duel through the eyes of Richard Dunwoody, who started the season as freshly crowned champion jockey and, despite all manner of setbacks, was still champion at the end of it.

Richard's own description of his turbulent season forms the main body of the text. Linking passages in italic type are by myself.

In Men and Horses I Have Known, *one of the greatest of racing books, George Lambton wrote: 'About the best thing in racing is when two good horses single themselves out from the rest of the field and have a long drawn-out struggle.' Substitute 'jockeys' for 'horses', and you have a description of the 1993–4 season.*

This book was begun before its ending could be known, and several people have provided invaluable assistance with a hectic project, notably Alison Barrow, Debbie Beckerman, Adam Sisman and Sheila Corr at Partridge Press, Peter Terry, Robert Parsons, David Hood of William Hill, Phillip Jones and Gillian Bromley.

On the day in March when we first met to discuss the project, just after Richard had returned from the hastily arranged skiing holiday in Val d'Isère, he was twenty-one winners adrift of Adrian Maguire. As we parted, having agreed to write the book together, I suggested: 'Now all you have to do is win the Grand National and win the championship.' My thanks to him for carrying out his instructions to the letter.

Sean Magee

1

LINING UP

Jump jockeys have falls, cars have punctures.

Just before the end of the 1992–3 season, soon after it was agreed that I would take over from Scu as first jockey to Martin Pipe, I was driving down to Martin's yard, near Wellington in Somerset. As I reached the junction where the M4 meets the M5 the car had a puncture on the slip road, and I couldn't get the wheel off: it turned out that it hadn't been greased properly and was corroded on. So I phoned the AA, and for what felt like about an hour and a half kept seeing the AA van appearing and disappearing around the roundabout ahead of me, trying to find out where I was! Various lorry drivers stopped and tried to help and we attacked the wheel with all sorts of hammers and mallets before the AA man eventually got down to me, but by then I was extremely late. I found myself wondering whether this episode wasn't some sort of omen for my new arrangement with Martin, whether someone up there wasn't trying to stop me going down!

For a jockey who admits to being just a little superstitious, the doubts were understandable.

In May 1993, at the age of twenty-nine, Richard Dunwoody was about to reach the very top of the tree by becoming champion jump jockey for the first time. To arrive at the pinnacle was a natural progression for the Ulster-born rider with racing in his blood – father George a successful amateur rider and trainer in Ireland, mother Gillian the daughter of Epsom trainer Dick Thrale. Richard first sat on a pony at the age of two, first led up a horse at a race meeting at Gowran Park at the age of seven ('Isn't he a bit young?', the stipendiary steward asked his father), and rode out at Newmarket for Ben Hanbury and Paul Kelleway before becoming Kelleway's pupil assistant. He then worked for a spell with trainer John Bosley near Bampton in Oxfordshire before moving down to join Tim Forster – 'The Captain' – at Letcombe Bassett, not far from his present home near Wantage.

Richard's first race under Rules was an amateur riders' handicap at Chepstow on 31 August 1982 – he finished second on 33–1 outsider Mallard Song – and his first ride over jumps at Stratford on 5 February 1983. The opening score in a winning tally that during the 1993–4 season would make him only the fourth jockey in jumping history to ride over 1,000 winners was on Game Trust in a hunter chase at Cheltenham on 4 May 1983.

Within just seven years he had become only the fourth jockey since the Second World War to have won the big treble of jump racing: Grand National, Cheltenham Gold Cup and Champion Hurdle. Following in the hallowed steps of Fred Winter, Willie Robinson and Bobby Beasley, Richard won the Grand National on West Tip in 1986, the Cheltenham Gold Cup on Charter Party in 1988 and the Champion Hurdle on Kribensis in 1990. He won a string of other big races, notably the King George VI Chase twice on the indomitable Desert Orchid, taking over the ride on the nation's favourite racehorse on the retirement of Simon Sherwood, and was closely associated with many other great chasers including Remittance Man and Waterloo Boy, the former trained by Nicky Henderson and the latter by David Nicholson, both men who played major parts in establishing Richard's reputation.

David Nicholson – widely known in racing as 'The Duke' – had himself been a top jump jockey before taking out his trainer's licence in 1968, the year after he had partnered the great Mill House to win the Whitbread Gold Cup. Son of Frenchie Nicholson, that fabled nurturer of young jockeys, The Duke soon established a reputation as a strong disciplinarian, but riding for his stable meant being associated with horses of very high quality.

Richard became David Nicholson's stable jockey in 1986 when Peter Scudamore moved to Fred Winter, and rode a string of big-race victories for the yard (then based at Condicote, near Stow-on-the-Wold in Gloucestershire), including Very Promising in the 1986 Mackeson Gold Cup, Charter Party in the 1988 Gold Cup, Waterloo Boy in the 1989 Arkle Chase, and Another Coral in the 1991 Mackeson and 1992 Tripleprint Gold Cup at Cheltenham.

For Nicky Henderson, his second retainer while contracted to Nicholson, he won the 1991 Arkle on Remittance Man and partnered horses of such quality that the combination of the

Nicholson and Henderson arrangements had helped him become the most successful rider in terms of prize money accrued for each of the three seasons before he finally landed the title itself.

During those three seasons – indeed, every season since 1985–6 – the champion jockey had been Peter Scudamore. Following Scu's sensationally sudden retirement at Ascot on 7 April 1993, the matter of who would replace him as main jockey for the trainer Martin Pipe became the hottest question in racing, and with good reason. Pipe had revolutionized the training of jumpers since taking out his licence in 1977. He was champion trainer for the first time in the 1988–9 season, and by the end of the 1992–3 term had occupied that position for five successive years.

The trainers' championship is decided on prize money won rather than on the number of winners trained, but it is in the latter category that Pipe blew the record books away. The first jumping trainer to send out the winners of 100 races in a season was Arthur Stephenson in 1969–70, but until Pipe the only trainer to have won the championship with over 100 was Michael Dickinson, with 120 in 1982–3. Pipe's first championship season in 1988–9 notched 208, followed by 224, 230, 224 again, and in 1992–3 a total of 194 winners.

The world of racing, like that of most sports, is a close-knit one, and Martin Pipe's extraordinary rise to the top from nowhere was accompanied in some quarters by a level of snobbery, envy, dark rumour and downright malice which did its perpetrators no credit. There was whispering – off the record, of course – of blood doping and other sinister practices, but gradually the results were allowed to speak for themselves, and those results did the world of good to the title prospects of his jockey.

In each of Pipe's five championship seasons except the latest his stable jockey Peter Scudamore had headed the riders' table, *and the job as number one jockey at Nicholashayne seemed to guarantee its holder the championship.*

But there were other considerations for Richard to ponder as he contemplated cutting his ties with The Duke, whose move to brand-new state-of-the-art stables at Jackdaw's Castle, near Temple Guiting in Gloucestershire, seemed certain to consolidate his position as trainer of the highest-class string around. Nicholson spelled quality, but Pipe, so the received wisdom went, meant quantity, and if Richard was to retain his championship quantity was precisely what he needed.

I'd ridden off and on for Martin over the years – my first winner for him was Au Bon at Uttoxeter in March 1989 – so I knew well enough that his horses are extraordinarily fit: in a race they just keep going when normally you'd expect them to fold up.

His secret weapon – not so secret, as it's been written about often enough – is the gallop at Nicholashayne, a single all-weather strip covering about six furlongs up an incline, quite stiff against the collar. Martin's theory of getting his horses fit is like interval training with an athlete: he sends each horse up the gallop, then we circle round at the top until the whole lot has come up, and head back to the foot of the hill before going up again.

The attraction of the job was that it meant a fresh challenge. Martin had been champion trainer for so many years, and barring accidents teaming up with him looked like the one way to be champion jockey again. But the idea that riding for him was putting quantity above quality was wrong; he had some very nice horses indeed down there. I was particularly looking forward to riding Rolling Ball, who had won the Sun Alliance Chase in 1991, Lord Relic, a top-class novice hurdler who looked sure to make a chaser, and of course Granville Again, the 1993 Champion

Hurdler. There was also the possibility that Carvill's Hill might yet make a comeback and become a Gold Cup horse, though in the event I never sat on him. I'd been scheduled to school him in Ireland when he was with Jim Dreaper, only for Jim to ring me when I was on the way to the airport to tell me not to come over as the horse wasn't right.

Miinnehoma had won the Sun Alliance Chase in 1992 but had not done much since. We were hopeful that he'd make his mark.

Obviously The Duke had plenty of class in his yard, with the likes of Wonder Man, Baydon Star, Carobee, Barton Bank and the 1992 Derby third Silver Wisp, not to mention old favourites like Waterloo Boy, but joining Martin represented fresh pastures, and I was ready to make a move.

I'd had a formal agreement with The Duke and with Nicky Henderson, but there was to be no such arrangement with Martin – simply an understanding that I would ride for him. The reward would be in the sheer quantity of winners. Such a system works both ways for both parties, and allows for greater flexibility than the standard trainer–jockey retainer.

If, at the opening of the 1993–4 season, Richard was unarguably top of the jump jockeys' tree, there was equally no dispute about the identity of the heir presumptive.

Adrian Maguire was twenty-two. Born and raised one of eight children of a green-keeper in Kilmessan, County Meath, he had cut his riding teeth in the argy-bargy of Irish pony racing, riding his first winner at the tender age of nine and clocking up over 200 before switching his attention to the point-to-point field. He was champion point-to-point rider in Ireland in 1991 while attached to the Limerick trainer Michael Hourigan, for whom he rode his first winner under Rules when taking a bumper – a National Hunt Flat race – at Sligo in April 1990.

Adrian's cherubic face, which cannot have changed much since that first race-riding triumph as a nine-year-old, initially came to the attention of English racegoers in sensational style at the 1991 Cheltenham National Hunt Festival – and ironically, given the events of the 1993–4 season, on a horse trained by Martin Pipe.

For Omerta to start at 11–1 in the Fulke Walwyn Kim Muir Chase for amateur riders on the opening day of the meeting must have had something to do with the presence of the completely unknown seven-pound claimer Mr A. Maguire in the saddle – and he was there only because the French amateur originally booked for the ride could not do the weight. Martin Pipe is not one to be especially sympathetic to jockeys putting up overweight, so the Frenchman was off and the Irishman put on.

The eleven-year-old Omerta had good form – he had won the National Hunt Chase at the Festival as a six-year-old when trained in Ireland by Homer Scott – but had been plagued by leg trouble for some seasons before joining Martin Pipe in 1990. In the Cheltenham race, his first run for his new trainer, Omerta launched Adrian's career with an emphatic twelve-length victory, and even better was to come when Maguire and Omerta turned in a barnstorming finish to beat Cahervillahow a short head in the Irish National at Fairyhouse the following month.

A distant third in that race was Toby Balding-trained Cool Ground, and it was to Balding's stable that Adrian came to pursue his career in England. He posted further notice of his meteoric ascent in the 1992 Tote Cheltenham Gold Cup when driving Cool Ground – a 25–1 shot – to a last-gasp short-head verdict over The Fellow; but there was a sour taste to the champagne in which that victory was toasted, one which would recur throughout Maguire's early years riding in England and make a big difference to the ultimate destination of the 1993–4 jockeys' championship.

You don't learn too much about finesse on the pony-racing circuits of Ireland, and Maguire's vehement use of the whip on Cool Ground incurred such official displeasure that he was suspended for four days. 'I was excessive,' he admitted, 'but you don't think of that during the Gold Cup and I wouldn't have won otherwise.' One man's squeamishness at over-zealous use of the stick is another man's admiration for a passionate will to win, but whatever your view of his style, there was no doubting that Adrian Maguire was heading for the top.

In 1991–2 he rode seventy-one winners, among them King Credo in the Imperial Cup at Sandown and Cool Ground in the Greenalls Gold Cup at Haydock Park as well as the Cheltenham Gold Cup, to finish eighth in the jockeys' table in his first full season riding as a professional. In 1992–3 he came third behind Richard Dunwoody and Peter Scudamore with 124 winners, including Sibton Abbey in the Hennessy, King Credo in the Tote Gold Trophy and Sirrah Jay in the John Hughes Memorial Trophy at Aintree.

By the end of that season Scu had retired, and Richard was, to borrow the name of a good David Nicholson chaser who donated two wins to the championship-winning total in 1992–3, King Of The Lot. But just as he had reached the top of the pile, here was a young pretender threatening to spoil the view.

Let battle commence – but before it does, a game of musical chairs. The key stables were Martin Pipe's and David Nicholson's. The key jockeys were Richard, Adrian and the brilliant Irish champion Charlie Swan, who had ridden four winners at the 1993 Cheltenham Festival. Who would end up with whom?

There was a tremendous amount of speculation about who would be taking over at Martin's. On Scu's recommendation I spoke to Martin a couple of times, and I also discussed the situation with David Nicholson and with Colin Smith – whose Ford Farm Racing owns The Duke's stables at Jackdaw's Castle – letting them know that if Martin wanted me I'd have to think very strongly about it. At the same time Martin was talking to various possible jockeys – notably to Adrian and to Charlie.

In the press, conjecture was rampant, if occasionally distracted by events on the Flat such as Zafonic's staggering victory in the Two Thousand Guineas. On 26 April, two days after Richard had won the Whitbread Gold Cup on Topsham Bay and thus become the first jump jockey ever to pass the £1 million mark in prize money earned by his mounts, the front page of the Racing Post *carried the headline: 'Dunwoody Offered the Job with Pipe'. The* Post's *report suggested that Richard would decide whether to take the job during the Punchestown Festival in Ireland that week, and David Nicholson was quoted as expressing himself with characteristic force: 'I don't want to sit around waiting for Martin Pipe until next July; I want to know shortly and Richard has said he will make a decision this week.'*

In the event the tie-up between Richard and Martin Pipe was not confirmed until the middle of the following week, when it was simultaneously confirmed that Adrian Maguire would be stepping into the Dunwoody shoes at David Nicholson's. Martin Pipe was enthusiastic about the arrangement – 'It's absolutely fantastic that we will have the champion jockey riding here again' – and Richard himself saw the Pipe connection as the key factor if he was to retain his championship.

Scu's retirement had thrown the cat among the pigeons, but when the feathers had settled and it was possible to see clearly again, the new arrangements offered intriguing possibilities for the coming season. A combination of Pipe and Dunwoody was the dream ticket for those looking for a regular supply of winners, while Adrian Maguire's teaming up with the talent flowing from David Nicholson's yard promised a succession of big-race victories; and there was the additional interest of how the energy of Maguire's sometimes over-enthusiastic style would be harnessed by The Duke. Richard was in no doubt about the powerful threat which the Nicholson–Maguire team posed to his title ambitions.

From the beginning of the season I knew that Adrian would be my main rival.

I'd not heard much about him before he won the Cheltenham race on Omerta, but he certainly stood out that day, and made an even greater impression when he short-headed Charlie and Cahervillahow in the Irish National. He made his presence felt over here soon enough, and he ended the 1992–3 season in tremendous style, largely because he was getting such good outside rides, particularly up north. This would be his first term as main jockey for a leading stable. He'd been connected to Toby Balding, of course, but most of his rides had come from smallish yards, and he clearly had very good outside contacts – which owed a lot to his agent Dave Roberts. I had Robert Kington acting as my agent, but I knew that the combination of Dave and The Duke would see Adrian riding a hell of lot of winners in the new season. I was right!

As an aperitif for the arrangement ahead, Richard rode several runners for the Pipe stable during the back end of the 1992–3 term, and the signs were good.

I had my best May ever – twenty-two winners, and twelve of those were for Martin.

At the end of the season Richard was champion jockey with 173 winners.

The break between the end of one jumping season and the beginning of the next is cruelly short for those closely involved in the sport. No month in 1993 did not include National Hunt racing – one season ended on 5 June, the next began on 30 July – and for the new champion, the few intervening weeks were hectic.

I like to be busy during the close season – press work, interviews, anything that's in any way constructive. Being the owner of a prominent false tooth, I even did an ad for Steradent.

Soon after the season had ended Carol and I grabbed a holiday in Barbados. There was a good group out there – Graham McCourt and his wife, Steve Smith Eccles, a couple of rugby players and a few footballers, including Niall Quinn. Usually in the close season I can let my weight go a bit, but Martin had been thinking of running a couple at Auteuil during our close season, and I knew I'd have to do ten-five or ten-seven on Lord Relic in the French Champion Hurdle early in July.

We got back on 27 June, and I went over to France to school Lord Relic and Sweet Glow for Martin at Maisons-Laffitte. Lord Relic, who had never been an exceptionally fluent jumper of English hurdles, jumped the French version – like miniature steeplechase fences – really well. The day of the race was extremely hot and in the conditions Lord Relic ran very well before fading three hurdles out to finish eighth behind François Doumen's Ubu III. Jamie Osborne on Sweet Glow finished behind us.

On returning from Paris it was time to organize the celebration party for winning the championship, which involved importing my favourite band, the Saw Doctors from Tuam in County Galway. The party was at the Farmhouse Restaurant at Frilford on 12 July, and the band came over in time for an impromptu performance the night before at The Fox and Hounds in Uffington – the pub run by Martin O'Halloran, who as a jockey had ridden that good chaser Bachelor's Hall. To have the Saw Doctors turn up there was a bit of a treat for the locals!

But with the new season only a few weeks away the raucous late nights had to be rationed, and it was important to keep fit.

The only activity which gets you really fit for race riding is race riding itself, and the first few outings of a new season are always hard work. Throughout the year I play squash when I can, and rely on regular use of the Equicizer to exercise the right muscles.

The Equicizer, which Richard had imported from the USA at the end of the previous season, is a sort of de luxe rocking horse which sits in an upstairs room of the Dunwoody house in the village of Sparsholt. Through an intricate pattern of springs, it replicates the motion of a galloping horse – complete with the nodding carriage of the head – in such a way that a few minutes astride it can have a similar effect on the leg and arm muscles as riding in a race.

I usually spend four or five minutes on it at a time – standing up on it, then getting down into the finish position for about thirty seconds, then standing up again, taking a short rest, and repeating the procedure. It's a lot more tiring than riding work, and excellent for the leg muscles, especially when building up fitness before the start of the season or coming back from injury.

But nothing beats riding a real horse.

Throughout July I rode out at Martin Pipe's once or twice a week to familiarize myself with his horses, and occasionally schooled for Martin and other trainers – Terry Casey, Charlie Mann, my neighbour Matt McCormack and Nicky Henderson, from whom I was hoping to get rides when Martin's horses were not engaged.

There was the usual progression of charity events, too, including a golf and polo match at Ringwood in Hampshire in aid of the Injured Jockeys' Fund, which was tremendous fun.

On 24 July I rode in Jersey, as I have done often over the last few years, and we stayed with Bunny Roberts, who had horses both with The Duke and with Nicky Henderson. The course at Les Landes is very sharp but rides well, and going there is always highly enjoyable. Carol and I had our honeymoon on the island, and Carol had her first race ride there.

Then it was over to Galway, one of the best of the Irish festival meetings. In the Galway Plate I rode The Gooser, who pulled up behind General Idea, ridden by Adrian.

But the new season in England was about to begin, and William Hill offered their prices on the jockeys' championship:

4–1 on Richard Dunwoody
5–2 Adrian Maguire
16–1 Peter Niven
20–1 Jamie Osborne

Whichever way you looked at it, this was a two-horse race.
A duel.

2

EARLY STAGES

Like a shy guest sneaking in at the edge of a party in full swing, the new jumping season arrives diffidently, and for plenty of followers of racing it is a while before they realize that it has turned up at all.

In 1993, as for the previous few years, the opening fixture on 30 July was at Bangor-on-Dee, the little racecourse near Wrexham notorious for giving nightmares to horsebox drivers who have mistakenly transported their charges to the other Bangor, in North Wales, and famous for not having a grandstand. It was the Friday of the Goodwood July Meeting – Glorious Goodwood – and with the flying filly Risky running in the Molecomb Stakes and Sheikh Mohammed's Teshami a well-backed favourite for the valuable Leslie and Godwin Spitfire Handicap, the racing pages had higher priorities than the opening moves in a jumps campaign which would run until the following June and would not gather any real momentum for at least another two months.

The opener on the first jumps card at Bangor was the Fred Archer Handicap Hurdle for conditional jockeys, and for half an hour the leading rider of the season was Alex Flannigan with an easy win on Little Big. Graham McCourt took the second on Moymet. Then Adrian Maguire put his name on the scoreboard with his first ride of the term, the odds-on OK Corral, trained by John White.

Richard Dunwoody's first mount of the new season came in the following race, a humble three-year-old claiming hurdle: Kesanta, a 7–1 chance against Mr Geneaology, 6–4 on to give Adrian Maguire a double with his second ride. We will be hearing more of Mr Geneaology later in the season. On the opening day he duly brought Adrian the double after a minor bumping match with Kesanta, who dived to the right away from the whip at the second last.

Richard's other ride at Bangor-on-Dee was sixth, while Adrian followed up his double with two placings.

There was a long long way to go, but first blood was to the challenger.

Two-nil.

The following day the attention of the jumping fraternity switched south to Newton Abbot in Devon. The West Country was Martin Pipe's true stamping ground, where the foundations of all those sensational seasons with Scu had been laid, and down here Richard would have runs on the board in no time.

Sure enough, his first ride for Martin Pipe that season provided his first winner.

Skipping Tim was a remarkable old horse. He had run in fifteen races under Rules before finally losing his maiden tag at the age of ten in a Newton Abbot selling chase in July 1989, after which he was bought out of Philip Hobbs's stable at the post-race auction by Martin Pipe for 5,500 guineas. By the time he ran at Newton Abbot on the second day of the 1993–4 season his winning total had shot up to twenty-four from sixty-one races – partnered in two of those victories at the back end of the 1992–3 season by Richard Dunwoody – and at the ripe old age of fourteen he was still going strong. Starting 7–4 favourite, he made all to win by three lengths from Karakter Reference.

Richard was off the mark; but Adrian won the next two races on Bondaid and Norstock to take a four–one lead before Richard pulled one more back with an easy win on 7–2 on chance The Executor for Martin Pipe in the fifth.

Four–two, though at this stage no-one was paying much attention to those totals. With ten months' hard graft ahead, there was plenty of time for the title race to develop.

Another Dunwoody–Pipe victory on the third day of the campaign – Merlins Wish at Newton Abbot on the Monday – brought the strike rate of the early runners for the combination to 50 per cent: three winners from six rides. Things looked set fair, but an early hint that all might not continue to go so smoothly came on the Tuesday at Exeter.

The nine-year-old gelding Celcius had won eleven races, and his odds of 6–1 on to beat two moderate opponents in a claiming hurdle seemed realistic enough.

I hadn't ridden Celcius before. In the paddock before the race I was told that he needed to be held up and was given orders to drop him in behind the other two and come late, but Martin also suggested that if the others didn't want to go on, I was to go ahead and make it. He meant that in those circumstances I should make the running and then drop in behind when I could, but as it turned out Celcius was so keen and gave me such a good feel that I just let him bowl along in front. Turning into the straight David Bridgwater on Emma Victoria swept past me and just hacked up. I'm sure that Celcius would have been beaten whichever way I'd ridden him and that his defeat was just one of those things, but there was undoubtedly a little friction in the unsaddling enclosure that day – though it was the only time all season that Martin and I had cross words.

A while later my ride on Celcius became a standing joke with Martin's assistant Chester Barnes, who would refer to it whenever he could: he'd always compare it with one of Scu's less fortunate rides for the stable, on High Knowl when he was beaten in the Tote Placepot Hurdle at Kempton in 1987. For Chester that Celcius race was a sort of low-water mark of my riding for Martin!

Two races later another Dunwoody–Pipe odds-on chance went down when Richard hastily dismounted from Millrous just after the fourth hurdle in the seller, though she walked sound again shortly afterwards. The Racing Post *the next day reported: 'Everyone has distinctly bad days but Martin Pipe and Richard Dunwoody will definitely want to erase yesterday's events at Exeter from their memories.' Too right.*

But there would be plenty of good days ahead, and an essential preparation for them at Martin Pipe's was schooling the young horses, teaching them to jump or giving them a refresher course.

We'd start them off small, and get their confidence by jumping them gently over logs or something else small but solid. Then we'd move on to try them over slightly bigger obstacles in the indoor school before taking them to the full-size hurdles on the all-weather gallop.

Horses vary in the amount of schooling they need: like children, some are fast learners, some take longer to get the hang of what is required. Some would be jumping well after three or four schooling sessions, while others would need twice that.

Usually I would go up the gallop once on a horse and pass it on to someone else if it was jumping properly: they would then continue to school it while I rode another. During one schooling session I'd often sit on ten or eleven different horses over hurdles and maybe three or four over fences.

And the jockey needed to be got into shape as well as the horses.

When I let myself go during the close season my weight usually goes up to about ten-ten, but when riding I try not to let it get above ten stone.

If I'm riding at ten stone I have to get my body weight down to about nine-ten – that allows for the weight of boots, breeches, colours, saddle and other tack such as girth and irons. The crash helmet is not weighed out or in, and we're allowed a pound for the back protector.

During most of the season I keep my weight at ten stone; Martin does not like overweight and I know I can lose three or four pounds by sweating if I need to. The danger is in wasting too hard: if you overdo it you make yourself weak, and though often you don't feel it during the race, when you pull up you can be totally drained, which isn't much good for your later rides that day.

When riding I try to keep to a reasonable diet. In the morning, a cup of coffee with milk (no sugar) and a couple of slices of toasted high-fibre bread with marmalade (no butter) – though if I'm doing light I might skip the toast. I might have a chocolate bar on the way to the races for the energy, and at the racecourse might have a sandwich and a cup of coffee with sugar. Then in the evening I'd have a light meal – chicken and a few vegetables – with a glass or two of white wine.

During the depths of winter the wasting can get to you, especially if you're having a bad run, and though I enjoy food I find that thirst from sweating can be a greater problem than wasting. I usually diet through the week then go out for a decent meal on Saturday night, and then sweat it off in the sauna at home if I have to do light on Monday. Many racecourses have their own saunas in the changing room, which means you can lose a couple of pounds just before a race if you need to.

My body tends to hold on to liquid when it has taken it in, and the only way to get rid of liquid in the short term are diuretics – which I've never taken – or sauna.

And so, with its ups and its downs for the reigning champion jockey, the infant season pottered through its first few weeks. While the attention of most racing fans was still firmly clamped to the Flat, to Lochsong and to Bob's Return, Richard clocked up the rides around the small jumping tracks, the 'gaffs' which form such an enduring element of jump racing's appeal – Plumpton, Worcester, Fontwell Park with its figure-of-eight steeplechase circuit, Newton Abbot again, Uttoxeter, Bangor-on-Dee again, Market Rasen, Hereford. On 20 August he was at Perth, a picturesque course in Scone Park and the most northerly track in Britain, where four rides brought him no winners but plenty of notice: acclamation for an extraordinary recovery after his mount The Rambling Man clouted the last fence in the novices' chase so hard that he was not able to repossess his reins before passing the post in third place, and a three-day ban for improper riding following his use of the whip on Clever Folly, narrowly beaten by Charming Gale in a handicap chase. Richard thus became one of the first jockeys to be punished under the fresh official Instruction regarding the whip, deemed to have transgressed by hitting Clever Folly out of his stride pattern, and with unreasonable frequency.

The difficult areas are the force with which the whip is used, and the frequency with which you make contact. You have to wave your whip to encourage your horse, not hit it at every stride. But the whip guidelines are certainly much better now than they were three or four years ago, and jockeys have accepted them and adapted well.

My use of the stick on Clever Folly appeared to be too frequent – the stewards' secretary said I hit the horse nine or ten times on the run-in – but Clever Folly and Charming Gale were racing so close together that I couldn't make contact most of the time. I didn't need to, as the old horse is a real battler. I actually only made contact about six times.

In terms of missed rides the Perth ban affected Richard little, as it ran from 29 to 31 August: although the middle day was Bank Holiday Monday (on which, in the event, Martin Pipe had no winners at Newton Abbot), the first was a Sunday and the third a Tuesday with no jump racing.

Perth was followed by a winnerless visit to Hexham, then on Sunday 24 August a quick flit over to County Kerry for two rides at Tralee, where the August fixture is now one of Ireland's great racing festivals. No winners, but good crack.

The following day I stopped at the motorway services near Exeter on my way to the races. Just as I was getting out of the car to fill up with petrol an old gipsy lady came charging up, offering to grant me any wish in return – of course – for crossing her palm with silver. Besides our health, my only wish was to be champion jockey again, but all I could find to cross her palm with was a five-pound note. Before I knew it she'd persuaded me to part with that fiver – and then another tenner – and as a good-luck charm she gave me a tiny seashell, which I kept in the car all season. One small seashell for fifteen quid – there were plenty of times through the winter when I wondered whether this wasn't the worst bargain of all time.

By the end of August the pattern which had been hinted at during the first few days of the season had seemed to establish itself in the shape of the jockeys' championship. Adrian Maguire had ridden seventeen winners, ten of them for Wendover trainer John White, who scorned the tradition of Martin Pipe carrying all before him in the early weeks to lead the trainers' table. Richard had had the same number of rides as Adrian – fifty-seven – but only eleven had won. Nearly one in three of Adrian's rides had scored, less than one in five of Richard's.

During September the quality of the racing gradually increased. There was still much to be done around the circuit of the gaff tracks (including northern outposts like Perth and Sedgefield), but at the end of the month came the first Cheltenham meeting of the season, around the recently established Park Course which saves the runners the trouble of going all the way to the top of the hill at the far end of the famous track. Any fixture at Cheltenham carries with it echoes of the Festival in March, and that first meeting of the autumn brings the seasonal reappearance of some of the better horses, proclaiming that the sport is about to become more serious.

There were lighter moments to be had first, and on 21 September Richard had three rides at another of the great Irish festival meetings, at Listowel – like Tralee, in County Kerry. The timing of the Listowel race week is said to give local farmers the opportunity to let their hair down after the harvest is in, and although Richard's rides – Loshian for Aidan O'Brien and What A Question and Plundering Star for Mouse Morris – did not yield his first Irish winner of the season, any visit to Listowel was great crack.

Back home, tongues were just beginning to wag. As September progressed, Adrian Maguire extended his lead, and the early spurt seemed increasingly less like a fluke which could be eroded once the Pipe stable hit full throttle. Sensing that Maguire's title bid was already firmly entrenched, the bookmakers took appropriate action. From betting 4–1 on Dunwoody, 5–2 Maguire at the start of the season, William Hill gradually shrank the gap in the odds during September, so that by the 21st of the month they were betting 6–5 on each of two.

Richard rode two winners for Martin Pipe at the Cheltenham fixture on 29 September – Tri Folene and Cloghlans Bay – but Adrian also scored that day on Mr Geneaology (whose main claim to fame in this story still lay months ahead).

By the end of September the score stood at Maguire thirty-four, Dunwoody twenty-two. It was still very early days, but was the championship so recently won already slipping out of Richard's grasp? He, for one, did not think so.

If I'd been expecting a really sensational start I'd have been disappointed, but I was content enough with eleven winners by the end of August. By the same point of the previous season

I'd had only six. At the end of September I'd ridden twenty-two winners, against twelve the previous year.

And yet I was perceived to be having a hard time, and it was that perception which was galling. I found myself thinking: I'm champion jockey, I rode 173 winners last season, but I'm having to prove myself all over again. That was difficult.

It wasn't so much a case of being in Scu's shadow in the Pipe job as the business of having to convince people of my worth all over again. That leads to trying too hard, and you find yourself starting to make mistakes, asking horses to do things they are not capable of.

Martin would often give very specific orders, and in the early weeks I would find myself trying to follow them too closely, so that I wasn't letting things evolve and riding my own sort of race, as I should have been doing. A jockey has to pay attention to the orders given, but has to be able to adapt to the circumstances of a particular race.

I know that the critics thought the first two months of the season were a time of great frustration and disappointment for me and for Martin, and it became rather boring reading about how we had both 'gone'.

In particular, it was aggravating to be beaten on horses which the betting suggested were strongly expected to win. The betting element should play no part in a jockey's expectation of how the horse will run, but you can't help it. If you're riding the favourite, you know that it's expected to run well, and if it loses you feel you've let people down. If the horse wasn't good enough and you've done your job properly, whether or not the horse was favourite should not affect you, but of course it does.

We weren't exactly flying, but compared with previous seasons I thought I'd made a perfectly good start.

That view was not shared by one observer in a Ladbrokes betting shop, who on 28 August had a £5 win double on Michael Stoute's Shaiba in the opening race at Goodwood and The Black Monk, trained by Martin Pipe and ridden by Richard Dunwoody, in the claiming hurdle at Hereford. Shaiba duly won at 11–2 but The Black Monk was beaten a length at 15–8 on. This reverse was all too much for the Ladbrokes client, who identified Richard as the villain of the piece and sent him a copy of the losing betting slip with an accompanying note:

WHAT KIND OF A JOCKEY ARE YOU?

ALL THE ODDS-ON OVER THE PAST WEEK.

I AM A PENSIONER AND I FOLLOWED YOU AND MR PIPE. 1–3, 8–15, 4–6, 4–5.

YOU MUST BE A BAD JOCKEY, ALL GOT BEAT IN JUST OVER A WEEK.

I HAVE HAD GOOD WINNERS COUPLED UP, I PUT THE ODDS ON TO PAY FOR MY TAX IN A BETTING SHOP.

I HAVE CALLED YOU SOME NAMES.

'I have called you some names.' But in his indignation the aggrieved punter forgot to sign his own.

3

GETTING INTO STRIDE

There are certain words and phrases which seem to crop up in any published profile of Richard Dunwoody: professional, single-minded, perfectionist, tunnel vision – even obsessive. The reasons for this choice of vocabulary are not hard to find. Take his record book. He logs every ride he has – be it Cheltenham or Sedgefield, in a Grand National or in Jersey – meticulously in a ledger, recording the performance of each horse he has ridden, together with recommendations to himself for the future riding of that horse. (It even includes details of all races in which Carol has ridden.) To study this document requires strong eyesight and provokes admiration for the sheer attention to detail which underpins his attitude to his job.

No entry exceeds one line, and each is scrupulously dated and numbered within each month. Each entry gives the name of the horse, trainer, racecourse and distance, position of horse in race, with winner (if not Richard's ride) or second (if he has won), prize money won (if appropriate) and number of runners, followed by a brief commentary – in his own version of the truncated phraseology of the form book – on how the horse ran, with notes about how it might be ridden in the future. For example, his last two rides in September 1993 were at Cheltenham:

Wont Be Gone Long – 'Led early slipped odd one dropping himself out and behind nearly ur 3rd ditch try visor'

Setter Country – 'Tucked in closed & ev ch fr 4 out blew up 2 out wknd run-in went right game mare'

There is no mention of a horse's price in the betting.

Beneath the list of September's rides is a summary of the month – rides, wins, seconds, thirds, fourths, unplaced, pulled up, unseated rider, ran out. (There would usually be a column for falls, but that month he had none.)

There is also a running total for the season, and, for good measure, a summary of his performances overseas.

Richard admits that he has always enjoyed keeping records, but behind the schoolboy zeal of this ledger is the conviction that the more he knows about each and every horse he rides, the better he will be when he rides it again – and the better equipped he will be to judge that horse's likely performance should he be riding against it.

It's also very useful to have proper information to hand if another jockey is riding a horse I've ridden and rings up to ask me about it, and sometimes people buying a horse at the sales might want my opinion if I've ridden it.

Professionalism in a jump jockey takes forms well beyond the elegance with which you present your horse at a fence.

Likewise, professionalism in a trainer reaches far beyond the contents of the feed bucket or knowing how many gin and tonics to pour down a prospective owner, and the Martin Pipe operation, like the Richard Dunwoody, is underpinned by the realization that the more information you can amass about each horse every time it runs, the better you will be able to carry out your job.

Martin Pipe requests that every jockey who rides for him fill out a short report form on the running of each horse, covering such matters as how the race was run, how the horse jumped and handled the going, tactical requirements, and recommendations about how it should be ridden in the future. Be it a selling hurdle at Taunton or the Cheltenham Gold Cup, the form must be filled in and given or faxed to Pipe.

The combination of Pipe and Dunwoody was a marriage of two perfectionists, two professionals striving to cover all the angles of their sport, to minimize the role of chance, accident or caprice.

There are other manifestations of the Dunwoody commitment, among them his decision early in October to consult the leading sports psychologist Peter Terry.

The notion of discussing with an expert the psychological aspects of their sport doubtless never crossed the minds of Bryan Marshall or Fred Winter, but the growth of sports psychology over the last few years has benefited a great many top players in a variety of fields. It offers a way of standing back from the physical activity of what you are doing and concentrating on the mental aspects as a way of improving overall performance.

Racecourse and press-box rumour later in the season hinted that turning to Peter Terry was Richard's response to a poor start to the season, but when he paid his initial visit on 11 October he was not particularly alarmed by how things were going. Adrian might have poached a lead, but there was still all to play for, and plenty of time in which to do so.

Peter Terry teaches sports science in the School of Physical Education and Sport at the West London Institute for Higher Education, and has been specializing in sports psychology for over a decade. He first made his reputation with tennis players, but has worked on the psychological aspects of a wide variety of sports and top sportsmen: 'My prime aim is to help people win, trying to pre-empt their problems and avoid them. I try to assess the needs of individuals, then either instigate an educational programme or tweak a few knobs here and there.' Richard Dunwoody gave Peter his first experience of examining the psychological side of being a jockey, and for Richard seeing a psychologist was a further way of ensuring that as he mounted his bid for the championship, all the angles were covered.

I'd read about Peter's work with the England cricket team, and thought that going to see him might help my riding. So I contacted him through Michael Turner, the Jockey Club's medical officer.

There's a lot more to riding horses than just the physical activity. As with any sport, a great deal is going on in the mind, and the ability to concentrate, to understand the downs of race riding and be able to cope with them, was vital.

Peter was not too familiar with the psychology of race riding, and having to explain about tactics and so on to a complete outsider was very revealing.

After that first visit in October I went to see him every two months or so, and each visit gave me a fresh angle on what I was doing in the saddle.

As far as Peter Terry was concerned, there were key areas for Richard to think about:

'We spent the first five minutes of our first meeting talking about Adrian Maguire. Richard was constantly relating what he was doing to what Adrian was doing, which was essentially a loss of focus and could clearly affect how he rode. He could miss the right stride going to a fence because he was too aware of what other people around him – notably Adrian – were doing.

'He was tense, fairly wound up about life generally, and the prospect of a very lengthy battle for the championship was not something he was approaching in a positive frame of mind.

'But he struck me from the word go as the consummate professional sportsman, one who left nothing to chance. His main need was concentration – focusing on what he should be doing during a race, and nothing else.

'So he had to relax, and reorientate himself. His attitudes had become negative, and he wasn't as decisive or assertive as he could have been. He was getting bogged down in non-riding issues.

'I gave him a relaxation tape – which he lost!'

The message with which Richard came away from that first meeting, and which was reiterated at their subsequent sessions throughout the roller-coaster of the season, was simple: stay focused.

But staying champion jockey was not all in the mind – there was plenty to be done in the saddle.

During the early part of October the jumping scene was still very much in the shadow of the Flat, then reaching its European climax with the Prix de l'Arc de Triomphe and the two big autumn meetings at Newmarket. For the most part, National Hunt racing was still taking place around the minor tracks, but for Richard a disturbing pattern was beginning to emerge.

Between the start of the month and Saturday the 16th – Cesarewitch Day on the Flat – he had only four winners from thirty-eight rides. Just five of those rides were for Martin Pipe. Meanwhile Adrian Maguire had increased the gap from twelve at the end of September to eighteen a little over two weeks later, and favouritism for the title had, in the language of the betting ring, flip-flopped, with William Hill having Adrian at 7–4 on by the middle of October and Richard out to 11–8.

At this stage Richard was not even a clear-cut second, as Peter Niven was snapping at his heels and Norman Williamson only just behind in fourth.

If the champion was beginning to worry, he had plenty of flying time in which to do so over the Cesarewitch weekend as he jetted across to New York to ride Highland Bud in the Breeders' Cup Steeplechase at Belmont Park on Long Island. The Breeders' Cup Steeplechase may have been the poor relation of Breeders' Cup Day on the Flat, the unofficial world championship of racing which takes place at a movable venue around the beginning of November each year, but the rewards for doing well in it were none the less considerable. To British racing fans it had in recent years become best known as a benefit for Toby Balding's individualist hurdler Morley Street, who won the race in 1990 at Belmont and in 1991 at Fair Hill, Maryland. But Morley Street was not the only horse to have won the race twice. Highland Bud, trained in the USA by Jonathan Sheppard, had won the Breeders' Cup Steeplechase as a four-year-old at Far Hills in 1989, the year he was sold out of David Nicholson's yard at the Doncaster Sales for 105,000 guineas, at that time the highest sum ever paid for a jumper in training. He repeated the Breeders' Cup win at Belmont three years later, and on both occasions was ridden by Richard Dunwoody, who had been instrumental in tutoring the young horse at David Nicholson's.

So Highland Bud had a special place in Richard's affections, a position not dented by his finishing second in the 1993 running, beaten eight and a half lengths by Lonesome Glory but picking up $60,000 in place money for his trouble. Ludlow to Belmont Park to Fakenham was Richard's itinerary that weekend, but the jockey's percentage of $60,000 helped combat the jet-lag.

Things picked up after his return from New York, with another ten winners in the second half of October bringing his score for the month up to fourteen, including a four-timer on the last day of the month at Warwick (Buglet, The Slater, Crystal Spirit and Parsons Green) to counter a Maguire treble on the same day at Wetherby (Durham Sunset, Ushers Island and Barton Bank).

But last year October had yielded 22, and only four of this year's October fourteen were for Martin Pipe. Why was the winner-producing factory not delivering the goods? Worse, was the title, supposedly guaranteed (barring accidents) by the link-up with Pipe, slipping away already? Richard tried to keep it all in perspective:

October had been a very quiet month for Martin the year before with Scu. Admittedly I'd been hoping for a better start, but I still wasn't too alarmed – though Adrian did seem to be getting rather a long way ahead.

At the end of October Richard had ridden thirty-six winners, but Adrian Maguire was on fifty-seven, and comparing their respective strike rates of winners to rides was a discouraging exercise. Adrian had won on 26 per cent of his rides, Richard just 18 per cent. At that point the trainer providing most of

Adrian's winners was John White, and Adrian's strike rate on White's horses was 44 per cent. In contrast, the strike rate of Richard riding Pipe horses was just 25 per cent.

The young pretender was getting clear of his field. The duel was becoming a damp squib.

November is the month when the jumping season, having waited patiently in the wings for so long, finally walks out to the centre of the stage and into the spotlight. The Flat winds down after the Breeders' Cup in the USA, and although there is all-weather Flat racing right up to the end of the year, interest in the sport on the level is by now minimal.

Between the beginning of the month and the morning of the Mackeson Gold Cup, the new season's first big race run at Cheltenham on the 13th, Richard added five winners from forty-four rides. In the same period Adrian Maguire put on ten winners from thirty-nine rides, and you do not have to be any great student of strike rates to see what was happening: the gap was not just getting bigger, it was beginning to yawn.

Richard had at least stayed clear of injury, but even that changed on 1 November. Manhattan Boy was a remarkable horse, living proof of the 'horses for courses' theory: all his fourteen career wins had been in selling hurdles at Plumpton. With Richard in the saddle, he was attempting to make it fifteen at the East Sussex track when he fell at the sixth flight.

I was pretty sore after that fall, though able to take my one remaining ride of the afternoon – Fred Splendid, which also fell. The following morning I went down to Martin's to school, and found that I couldn't get on the horse: I'd pulled a muscle. But after physiotherapy I managed to ride in the first at Exeter that afternoon and won – which made me feel a good deal better.

There were other problems in early November. Jump racing had been cringing with embarrassment since the fiasco of the Grand National false start the previous April, and there was a terrible sense of déjà vu when the twenty-runner Tote Silver Trophy at Chepstow on 6 November suffered similar shenanigans.

In the wake of the Liverpool episode, runners were now required to line up at a point a few yards behind the tape and walk in when under starter's orders, but as they moved forward on this occasion starter Simon Morant noticed that Simon Earle, behind the rest of the field on Andrew's First, was still adjusting his goggles. Morant yelled at the jockeys to wait but by then most were anticipating the start. The horses at the front became entangled with the tape, the worst sufferer being Jamie Osborne, who found himself dragged from his mount Leotard and then trampled on by Zamirah. Leotard was withdrawn from the race. Richard, riding Maamur for Martin Pipe, was not directly involved in the fracas.

Around this time everyone was approaching the start too quickly, and starters were simply not expressing their authority. After the Grand National everyone was very jumpy about starting procedures – jockeys as well as officials – and the starters were not showing as much confidence as they might have done that the new procedures were the right way to do it. It was as much about confidence as authority, but some of the blame must go to the jockeys, who must be able to control their horses. The best sort of start is the one where you all walk towards the tape. You don't trot, and anyone caught trotting should be brought back. If horses stand with their heads on the tape, as they did in the 1993 National, there's more chance of their getting kicked by another runner, and there's much more chance of a horse planting. The simplest solution is for the horses simply to walk towards the tape.

By the end of the season the problems with starts had mostly become a thing of the past, and starting was a great deal better than it had been a year before. Everyone involved had more confidence.

Richard did not ride at Cheltenham on the first day of the Mackeson meeting, the Friday, electing to go instead to Huntingdon, where he drew a blank from five rides.

That morning the front page of the Racing Post *highlighted Martin Pipe's 'unusually slow start to the jumps season', quoting the trainer's reaction to press speculation that there was a particularly bad virus affecting the horses: 'We've had a virus every year – there's always a virus about, but that's something you've got to live with. It's no more a problem this year than any other.' Ladbrokes reported that they were not betting on the trainers' championship, but had they been doing so Martin Pipe would have been 5–1 on or 6–1 on to retain his title, despite at that stage being only fifth in the table!*

Richard's ride in the Mackeson was General Idea, trained in Ireland by Dermot Weld, who less than a fortnight earlier had sent out Vintage Crop to become the first horse from outside Australasia ever to win the Melbourne Cup in a performance acclaimed as one of the greatest training feats in the history of racing. Running like Vintage Crop in the colours of Michael Smurfit, General Idea started a well-fancied 8–1 shot but was never in the race with a serious chance and weakened to finish a distant tenth behind Bradbury Star. 'V. flat', reads Richard's post-race comment in his record book.

The Mackeson was Richard's forty-seventh ride of the month in Britain. His forty-eighth was Oh So Windy in the second race at Leicester two days later. In between these two rides there was just time for a quick trip down to Camden, South Carolina.

First run in 1970, the Colonial Cup is one of the most important jump races run in the USA, and usually attracts a small contingent of British jockeys – and often a few British-based horses: among familiar names to have taken part in the race are L'Escargot (fourth in 1970), Inkslinger (winner in 1971), Soothsayer (winner in 1972), Captain Christy (fourth in 1975) and Grand Canyon (winner in 1976). In 1993 Richard was going over to ride his old friend Highland Bud for trainer Jonathan Sheppard.

It was all a bit hectic. General Idea in the Mackeson was my last ride of the day at Cheltenham, and it was then a mad dash with Jamie Osborne to get to Heathrow. Jamie's agent, the BBC commentator John Hanmer, drove us to the airport, where we joined up with Steve Smith Eccles, who'd been riding at Windsor that afternoon. We flew into JFK to be picked up by a taxi booked for us by Jonathan Sheppard which would take us across New York to our hotel near Newark, from where we were flying down to Camden early the following morning. It was late at night – very late British time – and we were all pretty tired after riding then flying across, so things in that taxi got a bit heated when the driver managed to get lost. He drove round and round as Eccy got less and less amused. In the end the driver managed to find the hotel, but it had taken two and a half hours to make what should have been a three-quarters of an hour journey.

Four hours' sleep, then we were up to catch the six o'clock flight down to Charlotte, South Carolina, from where we flew to Columbia.

Camden is a lovely course, almost spiral-shaped. You start on the inside and do one inner lap before moving to the outer. They only race there twice a year, and Colonial Cup day is like a huge picnic: loads of people, lovely warm weather, and a terrific atmosphere.

Sadly Highland Bud broke down very badly behind during the

race and initially I feared the worst, but his injury turned out not to be as bad as we first thought, which was a great relief. He was a smashing little horse, a top-class juvenile hurdler when with The Duke – second to Ikdam in the 1989 Triumph Hurdle – and I'd had some great rides on him.

Eccy won the race on Declare Your Wish, but he was still in a bad mood from the taxi ride, and it didn't help that we had no time to hang around in Camden celebrating his win, as we had to hare off to Charlotte to catch the six-twenty overnight to Gatwick, and get to Leicester, where I was due to ride Oh So Windy in the novices' hurdle.

One event we missed in Cheltenham on Mackeson night was the Champion Jockey's Ball, which as reigning champion I should have been at. I got a fair amount of stick in David Nicholson's new column in the *Racing Post* for not being there to collect my award – 'Dunwoody the Party Pooper' was the headline – but Carol accepted on my behalf, pointing out that when I was working with him The Duke had always instilled in me that work comes first. I'm told that got a cheer!

There was no time to feel tired. Four rides at Leicester on Monday, six at Newton Abbot on Tuesday, seven at Hereford on Wednesday, six at Wincanton on Thursday. Friday was the first day of a two-day fixture at Ascot, and with it came a major disappointment with the reigning Champion Hurdler, Granville Again. This was his seasonal debut, and there was some doubt about whether he was as effective over the Ascot trip of two and a half miles as he was over the championship distance of two, but it was none the less a blow that he went out so tamely in the home straight to finish fourth, nearly thirty lengths behind the winner King Credo.

That was the first time I'd ever sat on Granville Again, and my first outing on one of the stars of the Pipe stable must have added a little pressure. To be beaten was one additional turn of the screw when things were not going too brilliantly.

A bigger turn of that same screw must have been the way in which Adrian Maguire was clocking up the winners. He had won the Ascot race on King Credo, and another three winners the same day had brought his total to seventy-six, thirty-one ahead of Richard. Maguire was achieving a strike rate of 27 per cent. Richard's, at just 17 per cent, was the lowest of the five leading jockeys at that time, and Peter Niven in third place was just one winner behind him.

On the Saturday morning, the Racing Post *featured an article by Marcus Armytage – who had written* Hell for Leather *with Richard and as a Grand National-winning rider himself knew a bit about jockeyship – comparing the riding styles of the two duellists:*

'Dunwoody is more artistic than Maguire and shows more style and polish. He rides a sensible length, is tighter to the saddle and deeper into his horse and he has a slightly shorter hold on the reins. He has great balance on a horse and is rarely unseated. He is an organiser and probably thinks tactics through more, studies the form thoroughly, maybe he tries harder at knowing the facts.'

Marcus Armytage quoted John Hislop, famous amateur rider and perhaps the greatest theoretician of race riding:

'They are both very technically correct. They are equally resolute and efficient. Dunwoody is the more artistic. Neither makes tactical errors. Richard, in particular, always has his whip in the correct hand. I'd say there is nothing between them over a fence but it is easier for a small man [i.e. Maguire] to look better.'

The Post *article was evidence that the race for the jockeys' title was providing the dynamic to the jumping season. With*

*no exceptionally popular or charismatic racehorse in action –
Desert Orchid retired, and the return of Remittance Man no
more than a possibility – the main talking point of the season
was the Dunwoody–Maguire duel.*

*The Saturday that the article appeared was an important one
for jump racing, with the Grand National start at Aintree being
used for the first time since that fateful moment back in April.
The John Parrett Memorial Chase over one circuit of the National
course – named in memory of the Aintree clerk of the course
who had died suddenly the previous December – would see the
introduction of a new and supposedly fail-safe starting system.*

*Richard, however, did not expect to be at Aintree that after-
noon, as he was booked for six rides at Ascot. Then the weather
intervened, and he changed his plans.*

With a very heavy frost in the south, it looked odds-on that Ascot
would be called off. The formal announcement that the meeting
would not take place was not made until nine-thirty that morning,
but I'd already started to make my way up to Liverpool, hoping to
pick up some spare rides. Wont Be Gone Long, whom I'd ridden
– or not ridden! – in the aborted Grand National for Nicky
Henderson, was running in the Becher Chase, and I wondered
whether I could get onto him. I spoke to Nicky from the car while
driving up, and he suggested that as Mick Fitzgerald had ridden
him last time out he'd like him to keep the ride. I ended up riding
Hey Cottage for Ginger McCain. As it turned out I was lucky:
Wont Be Gone Long turned two somersaults for Mick, while I
had a good ride on Hey Cottage. The Becher Chase starts out by
the Canal Turn: Valentine's is the first, then we go back towards
the stands and do one complete circuit of the National course.
Hey Cottage slipped and nearly fell at the first and it took him
some time to get his confidence back, but after we jumped the

Chair fence in front of the stands his jumping improved and he eventually finished fifth.

Adrian had a nasty fall from Howe Street at the second last of the John Parrett Memorial, and another fall from Ushers Island at the same fence in the Becher Chase. He gave up the rest of his rides, so I came in for three spares, all Adrian's rides for The Duke – Master Jolson, who was last of three, Meleagris, who wouldn't start and was withdrawn, and Dan de Lyon, who was third.

The struggle to retain his title may have been hotting up, but as reigning champion Richard still had to endure the activities demanded these days of any sporting champion.

Hell for Leather: A Champion's Diary, *a chronicle of the events which led to his first championship in the 1992–3 season, had been published in October, and as part of the promotional round for the book Richard was invited to be 'God of the Day' on Simon Mayo's show on Radio One.*

'Is there anything left for you to achieve?' asked Mayo. 'What else is there for Richard Dunwoody to get excited about of a morning?'

Richard replied: 'Having been champion jockey last year, I'd quite like to do it again. It's going to be a little bit difficult this year – there's a young chap called Adrian Maguire . . .' As God of the Day, he chose Cindy Crawford and 'that woman from Baywatch' as heavenly bodies to have on his cloud, and Lester Piggott to become a saint.

Towards the end of November, the week before the Hennessy, I flew over to Ireland to school Flashing Steel for John Mulhern. Flashing Steel is an exceptionally promising young chaser owned by Charles Haughey, former Taioseach, and I schooled him round the racecourse at Navan.

I'd never won the Hennessy, but I had a high opinion of Rolling Ball, my 1993 ride for Martin. He hadn't run for two years but he'd pleased me in his work at Nicholashayne and I was hoping for the best. I suppose he may have been a bit fresh after such a long layoff, but we got no further than the third fence. He just galloped straight into it, and that was that.

That fall apart, Hennessy day was not at all bad. I won the opener on Egypt Mill Prince for Jenny Pitman, then in the second I had my first important win of the season for Martin when Bold Boss beat Adrian and Winter Squall in the Gerry Feilden Hurdle.

November was coming to an end with Adrian stretching his lead, and for Richard the pressures were growing as the Pipe stable remained in the doldrums.

There was a lot of tension and some friction as we just couldn't shake off the latest virus. Some of the owners were getting impatient (a couple even wrote to Martin to complain about his new jockey), the press was constantly going on about the lack of winners, and there were even times when I found myself wondering just how long my relationship with Martin would last.

Troubled times, but Richard could still have his moment in the limelight. In the River Severn Handicap Hurdle at Worcester on 29 November, he was riding Uluru for trainer Chris Nash. Approaching the second last hurdle he moved up.

I'd been tracking the leaders and then pushed him into the lead, and at the second last he just guessed and went too long. We were beginning to race flat out at that stage and I didn't have much contact with his head, so I left him to make up his own mind and he paddled straight into it. I half expected him to fall, but he was instantly back into his stride, and as he regained his momentum I went backwards, slipping the reins to the buckle end, and very nearly went out the offside back door. I yanked the reins to get back into the plate, and nearly went out the nearside front door as my saddle – the lightest I have – had started to slip round. I was just able to right myself off his neck and get back in contact with him before the last – which he pinged. On the run-in I didn't have to be too hard on him to win by five lengths. These incidents always look very spectacular, but there's a bit of luck involved. Sometimes you manage to get back, sometimes you don't.

The Chaseform Note-book *was appreciative of what was being hailed as the recovery of the season, noting how Uluru 'made an almighty mistake and was all but down, but his jockey made a miraculous recovery. Though he looked to have lost his chance, he found extra on the run-in to regain command and win going away. A truly marvellous performance.'*

Down but not out. By the end of the season Richard Dunwoody's recovery on Uluru at Worcester was to seem like a prophecy.

4

THE BLEAK MIDWINTER

December dawned with Adrian Maguire twenty-seven winners clear of Richard, the scores seventy-nine to fifty-two. The month was not very old before both were in hot water over the still controversial matter of race starts.

There were eight runners in the Barry D. Trentham Challenge Bowl at Uttoxeter on 2 December. Richard was riding Freeline Finishing for Nicky Henderson and Adrian was on David Nicholson's good chaser Bishops Island, and the pair, along with two other runners, pinched a flying start by approaching the tape at a canter while three of the other runners were sideways on behind the rest of the field. No false start was called and eventually Nevada Gold, one of those left twenty lengths or so, pulled his way back into the race and ran out a convincing winner. Adrian was third on Bishops Island and Richard fifth.

A stewards' inquiry was called, and the ruling handed down that Dunwoody, Maguire and the riders of the other two who had made a quick break – Peter Niven and conditional jockey Richard Davis – were guilty of 'disregarding the starter's instructions and anticipating the start'. Each was fined £110.

Richard accepted the decision, though he disagreed with it:

It was my job to get a good start, and my horse, along with the others, just cantered for a stride or two when approaching the tape. I'd said after Chepstow that starters should show more authority and I stood by that view after Uttoxeter.

Two days later Adrian went to the big meeting at Sandown Park and continued his steamrolling run by winning the first three races on Barton Bank, Super Coin and Baydon Star. Meanwhile at Chepstow, Richard landed the opener on Bond Jnr and in the Rehearsal Chase came second on Riverside Boy behind the 1992 Grand National winner Party Politics, with the 1993 Gold Cup hero Jodami disappointing in third place. Dark rumours were abroad of Jodami's having been got at but nothing was ever proved, and for Richard the encouraging run of Riverside Boy in such exalted company augured well for a return visit to the course for the Coral Welsh National at the end of the month.

Another of Richard's mounts that day was Monsieur Le Curé for John Edwards. He fell three out in his race but would end the season as the best staying novice in the country.

That Saturday's results put Maguire on eighty-seven and Dunwoody on fifty-five, and a sign that the jockeys' championship was as good as over came with another revision of the William Hill odds: Maguire 5-1 on, Dunwoody 3–1 against.

After Chepstow we went up north to stay with Niall and Gillian Quinn, and took in a Saw Doctors concert in Manchester.

The next day – the Monday – Celcius was running at Ludlow. I was due to be going to London for the Derby Awards lunch, the annual bash of the Horserace Writers' Association. I only had one ride lined up at Ludlow and tried to persuade Martin to let me ride Celcius. Since I'd got beaten on him that day at Exeter at the beginning of the season he'd been running in amateur and conditional jockeys' races, in which he'd been very well partnered by Tom Dascombe and Nick Moore, and Martin thought it only fair to leave Tom on the horse. However, Martin eventually agreed to put me back on him at Ludlow, and he duly won, together with Chris Nash's West Monkton in the first.

Celcius was Richard's second winner of the day and his thousandth winner worldwide – 965 in Britain, including those as an amateur, twenty-five in Ireland, four in the USA, three in Jersey, two in Belgium and one in Australia.

If the thousandth winner was a milestone worth remembering, that afternoon has a less pleasant memory for Richard: it was at Ludlow that day that he finally broke with his agent Robert Kington.

Jockeys' agents, who book their clients' rides for a percentage of their riding fees, plus a cut of winnings, are a comparatively recent phenomenon in racing. Nowadays most big-name jockeys recognize that having a good agent is as important as being attached to a top stable: not only will the agent's skill and sheer energy pick up a good number of 'outside rides' for his jockeys – that is, rides for trainers with whom that jockey is not normally associated – but the best agents are such good students of the form book that they will be able to home in on the plum spare rides. They are looking for winners, not just riding fees.

As a young jockey in Fred Winter's Lambourn yard, Robert Kington had been closely associated with that remarkable chaser Sonny Somers, who in 1980 notched his last win at the age of eighteen. Robert had been Richard's agent for nearly six years when the split came.

Robert had done a very good job for me, but by December it just wasn't working out. We both realized it, and accepted that a break was inevitable.

When he was working for me I'd be in touch maybe six or seven times a day on average – four times in the morning discussing possible rides for the next day's racing, and at least twice in the evening to look further beyond that.

After the break with Robert I acted as my own agent for a while, so it is with some authority that I can say it's a desperate job. The key is constant contact with trainers. The jockey may speak to some trainers, the agent to others, but the agent always has to keep on the right side of the key people. From crack of dawn the agent has to be on the phone constantly trying to liaise with trainers. Sometimes two or three trainers want the same jockey, and then the agent has to help him choose. Strings are being pulled, favours called in from way back.

I was well aware that a big difference between how I had gone through the first few months of the season and how Adrian had was down to his agent – Dave Roberts, then considered by many jockeys to be the best in the business. He is especially well connected up north, where Adrian was picking up a great many spare rides. I found that I was playing second fiddle to Adrian for the spare rides, and it was very frustrating. There was one occasion in the 1992–3 season when I went up to Cartmel for one ride and Adrian had five – though in the event I ended up riding three of his as he'd been injured.

After I'd made the break with Robert I decided that I wouldn't replace him immediately but would book all my own rides, as I didn't want to rush into anything. This extra burden just added to the aggravation through December. Martin wasn't having too many runners, so I depended a great deal on outside rides. I found myself on the phone non-stop.

With Richard having an eventful afternoon at Ludlow, Carol Dunwoody attended the Derby Awards lunch in London and accepted the top jump jockey award on his behalf. The following day he went to Plumpton for three rides (no winners), but could have been elsewhere.

I'd been awarded the MBE in the Queen's Birthday honours in June, and they offered me 7 December as a date for the investiture at Buckingham Palace, but I asked if it could be deferred as there might have been winners to be ridden at Plumpton.

Jump racing had now entered one of its most enjoyable and hectic phases, with every weekend bringing a big meeting, and the Boxing Day fixture at Kempton Park just a couple of weeks away. A fortnight before the Christmas weekend came two days of high-class sport at Cheltenham.

Flashing Steel ran very well to win the big chase on the Friday from Ushers Island and Topsham Bay. On the Saturday I had what looked to be some pretty good rides, but Granville Again fell at the fourth in the Bula Hurdle, and then there was the Tripleprint Gold Cup.

Martin's entry in this was Fragrant Dawn, though Jenny Pitman had offered me the ride on Egypt Mill Prince if I was free. I'd won a nice race on Egypt Mill Prince at Newbury on Hennessy day, and Jenny had said that she needed to know by the Tuesday before Cheltenham whether I'd be able to take the ride. Martin's view was that Fragrant Dawn would get the trip of just over two and a half miles, though the horse had never won over much more than two miles and I wasn't so sure. So I rang everyone I could think of, including Mark Dwyer, who used to ride Fragrant Dawn when he was trained by Jimmy FitzGerald, and Paul Holley, who had ridden him for David Elsworth: they all said there was no way he'd get the trip, and so I made my mind up to go for Egypt Mill Prince.

Ridden by Declan Murphy, Fragrant Dawn won this valuable race by three lengths from Young Hustler. Egypt Mill Prince was a distant ninth after hitting the last.

It was just one of those things. You make decisions on the best evidence available, and sometimes you're wrong. You try to cover all the angles, but you can't always be right. I suppose that four or five years ago I might have taken the result far worse than I did, but I like to think that generally I have a better attitude than I did then.

None the less, it was not pleasant to learn in John Garnsey's column in the *Daily Express* on the Monday that I would be out of a job by Christmas.

On the whole I get on very well with the press: they have their job to do and I have mine. But when they start publishing stories like that, which have no basis whatsoever in the facts of the situation, it does get to you.

Over the next few weeks I was interviewing potential new agents. I had plenty of letters from complete strangers, some of whom had worked in racing, offering their services, but I was aware that the key qualification was someone who knew and got on with the trainers, and I was prepared to wait until the right person came along.

On 13 December it was announced that bookmakers William Hill would be sponsoring the 1994 Flat jockeys' championship and the current jump jockeys' title, which added a significant boost to the profile of both. Hitherto there had been an informality about the titles – there had been debate, for instance, over whether all-weather racing should be included – but with the first sponsorship came an official arbiter in the shape of the statistics published by the Racing Post.

Hill's would give a trophy to the winner of each title – plus an award for the top apprentice on the Flat and top conditional jockey over jumps – and donate £10 for every winner ridden by the champion under each code to the Injured Jockeys' Fund and the Jockeys' Association.

At this stage the outcome of the first sponsored jump jockeys' title seemed tied up, and the identity of the first official champion obvious, for Adrian Maguire had hit a purple patch. By the end of the Cheltenham meeting on 11 December the score was ninety-three to fifty-eight: a gap of thirty-five.

The weekend before Christmas was Ascot, but I had a disappointing day: Capability Brown ran poorly behind Young Hustler in the big chase, and Lucky Again buried me at the third in the two-mile chase. Various people told me I was mad to ride him in a top-class race when he had very little chance, but no harm was done.

When racing shut down for its Christmas break the gap between the two leading jockeys was still thirty-five, with the score at ninety-eight to sixty-three. Adrian had narrowly missed breaking Peter Scudamore's record of the fastest century, which Scu in 1988 had clocked up on 20 December.

On the Thursday before Christmas the jumping fraternity let its collective hair down for the Jockeys' Dance at the Farmhouse Restaurant at Frilford, near Wantage, and on Christmas Eve the Dunwoodys hosted a party at their house on the edge of Sparsholt, where the guests included Adrian Maguire and his girlfriend Sabrina. Those who insist that hostility underpins the rivalry between the two jockeys must take into account their regular and continuous social relationship.

I had to do light on Beyond Our Reach at Kempton on Boxing Day so I couldn't go mad on Christmas Day. I had a bit of turkey with some vegetables, then sweated off the excess in the sauna. On the twenty-sixth – which was a Sunday, with no racing in England – I flew over to Dublin for three rides at Leopardstown and won the Dennys Gold Medal Chase for Jim Bolger on Chirkpar, who was handed the race when Mubadir fell at the last.

Then it was Kempton Park on Boxing Day – always a huge crowd, great atmosphere, and for me special memories of winning the King George twice on Desert Orchid. People talk about pressure in sport, how it's all to do with expectation, and this was never better illustrated for me than when riding Dessie. So much was expected of him, so many people were willing him to win, that there was a real burden of responsibility in being his rider – and a real sense of relief each time we returned to the Kempton unsaddling enclosure having won the King George.

Dessie has retired but the Kempton buzz on Boxing Day is still huge. In 1993 I had several good rides, but nothing went according to plan.

In the first, the novice hurdle, I rode Duke Of Eurolink: it was his first run over hurdles, and he went well to finish fifth behind Shujan. The second was the three-mile novice chase, and here, riding the hotly fancied Coulton, I had my worst fall of the whole season. From the start he had been very keen and hadn't been too clever at getting in close to a fence, and going into the first down the back straight I squeezed him up to try to go a little bit long, and he put down and galloped straight into it. On television it looked as if he'd landed right on top of me. In fact he'd just missed me, and I was lucky to get away with just a severe shaking.

I have felt better in my life than I did after that fall, but I was able to take the ride in the next on Honest Word, who had not run for nearly two years but performed quite well to come sixth behind Child Of The Mist, Adrian's ninety-ninth winner of the season.

In the King George VI Chase I rode Rolling Ball, hoping to get further than we had in the Hennessy. But he ran extremely disappointingly, making a mistake at the fence in front of the grandstand first time round and then dropping out very quickly. I pulled him up before the seventh last.

The King George was won by Barton Bank, trained by David Nicholson and ridden by Adrian Maguire, after a thrilling battle from the last fence with Bradbury Star and Declan Murphy. It was Maguire's hundredth winner of the season, though the gloss of a marvellous race was somewhat tarnished by both jockeys receiving two-day suspensions for hitting their mounts with unreasonable frequency. Declan Murphy subsequently appealed against his ban and won his case, but the race yet again focused attention on the problem of interpreting and implementing the Jockey Club Instruction on whip use.

The clamour to canonize Adrian Maguire, which had been gradually gathering momentum through the early months of the season, had reached a new pitch with his surge of winners during December; and as he passed the post after a brilliant ride on Barton Bank and raised his arm in a victory salute, the clouds above Kempton Park opened and the halo was lowered into place. The small matter of the whip apart, this boy could do no wrong, and to ride his one hundredth winner for The Duke in the King George must have been planned in heaven.

David Nicholson himself would have agreed, declaring: 'I have only been in racing since 1945 but Adrian is the best I've seen. That's not an accolade – it's the truth.' To be hailed as the best ever seen by The Duke, however, rang a bell with Richard:

David said that Adrian was the best he'd ever seen. He said that about me three years ago – and I'm sure he's said it about Scu as well! But for Adrian to be getting all that adulation was not going to distract me. I knew The Duke well enough, and I also knew that to have that sort of public backing is a wonderful fillip for a jockey working for him: you tend to ride with a lot more confidence if you know that your trainer is completely behind you.

Nor could I let it bother me that the King George had been won by a horse I could have been riding had I stayed with The Duke. This sort of thing was bound to happen. Barton Bank may have won the big race one day, but I was already looking forward to the ride on Riverside Boy for Martin in the Welsh National the next day. You can't have it both ways.

And sometimes in jump racing, you can't have it at all.

In the race after the King George I rode a very nice novice chaser named Dante's Nephew for Matt McCormack. Matt is a neighbour in Sparsholt and I ride work for him regularly. I'd schooled Dante's Nephew several times and he was shaping up into a very good chaser. He'd had one run over hurdles, in which he was ridden by Dean Gallagher, and the Kempton race, the two-and-a-half-mile Wayward Lad Novices' Chase, was his first steeplechase. We were all looking forward to a good run.

He jumped well in the early stages, and coming past the stands first time round I was quite happy with him. But at the water jump, the first on the stretch going away from the stands, he was very awkward. He dropped his hind legs in the water and The Glow jumped on top of us. Both horses ended up on the floor, but it was the end for Dante's Nephew: he'd broken his back and was put down.

It is sickening when a horse is killed in a race, but as a professional jockey you just have to accept that it's part of what you do and harden yourself to it. The person I really feel sorry for in those situations is the lad or lass who looks after the horse, and for me the worst sight in racing is to see the lad or girl rushing up the track in tears to get to their injured charge. They're the ones who get closest to the horses, they're with them every day, and with some of those old chasers they might have a relationship which has been built up over seven or eight years, or even more.

It may sound brutal to say so, but the jockey just has to carry on and think about the next race.

In Richard's case on Boxing Day, the next race was the Tripleprint Handicap Hurdle.

I rode Beyond Our Reach for Ron Hodges. We were run out of it after the last by Lorna Vincent on Peatswood, and if anything I was more frustrated by that result than by Barton Bank's winning the King George!

Boxing Day may have been the high point of Adrian Maguire's season, but the following day was one of the best for Richard, with Riverside Boy winning the Coral Welsh National at Chepstow.

It was a very straightforward ride – all I had to do was keep him jumping and keep him balanced. He just galloped them into the ground, and had the race well won early in the straight. In the end he came home twenty lengths clear of Fiddlers Pike and Rosemary Henderson, but there was one little aspect of Riverside Boy's performance which slightly bothered me, and I told Martin after pulling up that the hardest part of the race was getting him round that bend just past the winning post. He jinked there, and looked out at the racecourse stables.

The Welsh National was my first really big win for Martin, and it was good to get that one under my belt, especially as he'd won the race so many times: Riverside Boy made it five out of the last six years.

The year ended with quieter meetings at Stratford (two winners), Taunton (none) and Leicester (one). As Auld Lang Syne was rung out Adrian's score was up to 105, Richard's at sixty-seven. The lead was now thirty-eight.

5

TURNING THE CORNER

For Richard, the greeting 'Happy New Year' had a hollow ring.

I don't think I'm going to ride on New Year's Day next year. A few years ago I got a very bad neck injury at the New Year meeting at Cheltenham, aggravating a knock I'd had a few days before at Leopardstown. I had about four weeks off. Another year I rode Mulloch Brae at the same meeting at Cheltenham, and she nearly wiped me out. In 1993 it was Winabuck who all but did me in at Windsor on New Year's Day. And then in 1994 I had that day at Newbury.

It was the first race of the afternoon. Adrian was riding

Winter Forest for The Duke, I was on Supreme Master for Richard Hannon. Richard is better known as a trainer on the Flat than over jumps, but he sends a few hurdling, and Supreme Master had some useful form on the level. He was favourite here, and travelling to the last vying for the lead with Adrian I was going slightly the better. A good jump at the last flight should have settled it, but I asked him to go too long, and he just didn't get the height. He stepped at it, hit it hard, and I managed to bail out. Another day I may have stayed on him – it was comparable with Uluru's mistake at Worcester.

Adrian was riding a lot of winners at this time and after the King George on Barton Bank had been built up as the new sporting superstar, and to present him with yet another winner was pretty galling. After the race I had to go out and receive an award for being top jump jockey at Newbury in 1993 – there weren't too many happy photographs taken at that presentation.

I was furious with myself for not staying on board Supreme Master, my shoulder was still sore after the Kempton fall from Coulton on Boxing Day, and Adrian was too far ahead. To make matters worse, I had no agent and seemed to be spending all the time on the phone booking my rides. It was a very dark time, and I was about ready to be carried away by the men in white coats. I just felt like giving up.

I left Newbury in a filthy temper. By the time I got home I was really wound up, and Carol bore the brunt of my depression. We had a flaming row, I threw a few things into a bag, and stormed into the car. I headed east up the M4, determined to get to Heathrow and book a flight to anywhere, just to leave it all behind for a few days.

Driving up the motorway I gradually calmed down, and thought better of the idea at junction 11, where I turned round and drove back home. Carol had gone to bed by the time I returned, so I cooked myself some supper, downed a couple of scotches, and cooled off.

The next day was Sunday – just as well after the evening before – but there was hard graft to be done sorting out rides for the Monday, the Bank Holiday. Nicky Henderson wanted me to go to Cheltenham to ride Barna Boy and Everaldo, while Martin had a few runners at Exeter. Martin left me to make up my own mind, so I ended up riding at Cheltenham – a third, three fourths and a faller (Gay Ruffian for Martin) from five rides. Adrian had a double at Cheltenham that day, and down at Exeter Martin had four winners. I thought perhaps I should have kept driving to Heathrow.

There was no jump racing on the Tuesday – Newton Abbot was abandoned because of waterlogging – but it was a turning point in the season, the day when Robert Parsons started work as my new agent.

About three weeks earlier the press had been saying that Robert was about to become my agent, though I'd never actually spoken to him then, let alone met him. I'd got in touch with him in late December and had been discussing possibilities with him, and the day after that awful Newbury meeting we agreed terms. He hadn't handled any jump jockeys before but was working for Richard Quinn on the Flat and came highly recommended as just what I wanted – sharp, experienced, knowledgeable, and very good with trainers.

At that stage the gap between myself and Adrian was up to forty-two. Too many of Adrian's winners for my liking were coming from outside rides booked by Dave Roberts, and I needed someone who could match Dave's efficiency. Robert Parsons had done a great job for Richard Quinn since starting to book his rides a few years ago when Richard was passed

Not much good for my image as shy, reserved Richard Dunwoody: 'Corky' Caulfield, Secretary of the Jockeys' Association, and Carol join me in assisting the Saw Doctors at the party in July 1993 to celebrate my first jockeys' title.

Off the mark: my first winner of the 1993-94 season – Skipping Tim at Newton Abbot on 31 July 1993.
Colin Turner

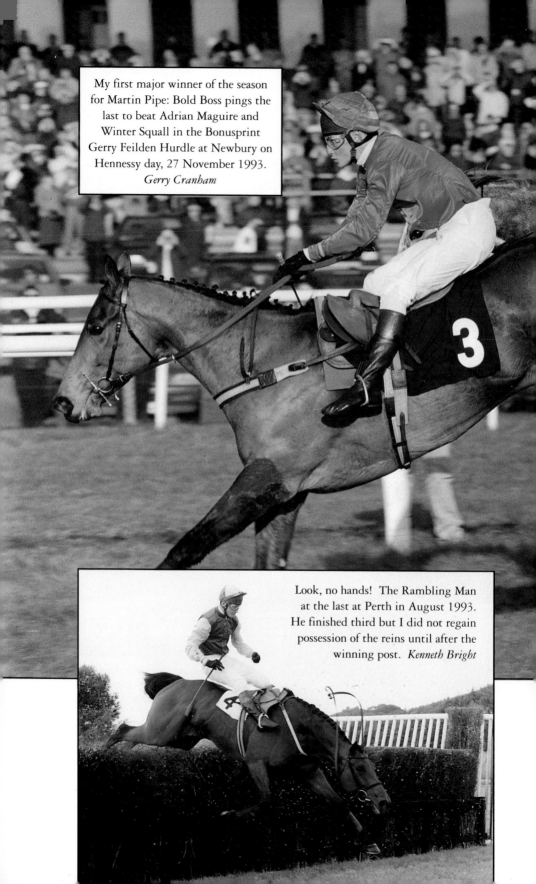

My first major winner of the season for Martin Pipe: Bold Boss pings the last to beat Adrian Maguire and Winter Squall in the Bonusprint Gerry Feilden Hurdle at Newbury on Hennessy day, 27 November 1993. *Gerry Cranham*

Look, no hands! The Rambling Man at the last at Perth in August 1993. He finished third but I did not regain possession of the reins until after the winning post. *Kenneth Bright*

One way to get a better view of where Fragrant Dawn has gone in the Tripleprint Gold Cup at Cheltenham on 11 December, as Egypt Mill Prince blunders at the last. *Gerry Cranham*

The Coral Welsh National, December 1993: Riverside Boy leads Fiddlers Pike (left) and Cool Ground on the first circuit. *George Selwyn*

My 1,000th winner in Britain, as Flakey Dove attacks the last at Cheltenham in January. Sweet Duke (Carl Llewellyn) glances across. *Les Hurley*

A nasty-looking fall from Ambassador at Kempton Park in January, but we were both unscathed. *Carol Dunwoody*

Another great moment the same day at Cheltenham: The Duke dances a jig as Waterloo Boy comes in after beating Richville by a head. *Les Hurley*

Here's looking at you, Ed. Lord Relic gazes straight down Ed Byrne's lens on the way to post before his first chase, at Lingfield Park in February. *Ed Byrne*

The Nottingham incident. Enough said! *Express/S.I.S.*

One of the great comebacks of the season: Remittance Man about to collar Declan Murphy and Deep Sensation at the last in the Emblem Chase at Kempton Park in February.
Carol Dunwoody

On the piste during Cheltenham week, with Mark Low (left) and Dermot Supple.

in association with

RACING POST

At the 1993 Jockey of the Year Awards – the 'Lesters' – in March 1994. Standing are Warren Marston (Conditional Jockey of the Year), Jason Weaver (Apprentice of the Year), Peter Scudamore (joint winner of Personality of the Year), Diane Clay (Lady Jockey of the Year), and Graham Bradley (Riding Achievement of 1993, on Morley Street at Aintree), with, in the front row, Adrian Maguire (Jockey of the Year), the Jump Jockey of the Year, and Frankie Dettori (Flat Jockey of the Year and joint winner of Personality of the Year). *Mel Fordham*

One of my best rides of the season: Docklands Express in full flight in the Martell Cup at Aintree on 7 April. *George Selwyn*

over for the Fahd Salman retainer, and the results spoke for themselves: Richard's first century in 1992, and a personal best of 125 winners in 1993.

Robert Parsons had been in racing for years, first with trainer Henry Candy – for whom Richard's wife Carol regularly rides out – and then for six years as agent to Tony Clark before moving on to book rides for Richard Quinn. After coming to an arrangement with Richard Dunwoody, he found his new charge 'desperate to be champion jockey again', and set about establishing a modus operandi which would work to their mutual benefit. It was agreed that his work for his 'new' Richard should never be allowed to interfere with his duties for Richard Quinn, and the matter of when an agent acting for one top-class Flat jockey and one top-class jump jockey might be expected to take a holiday was eventually decided. (The answer was January 1995.)

The appointment of Parsons added an intriguing sub-plot to the drama of the duel. It was widely acknowledged that in Dave Roberts Adrian had a formidable weapon on side, but one which would now be matched by a big gun from the world of the Flat. With both men burning up the telephone wires to book rides for their clients, each of the protagonists had a major second in his corner.

It was a huge relief to get a new agent. I'd had only a month without one, but it felt like a year. During that period, I was never off the phone. If I was going down to Martin's I'd be calling round about rides before riding out, sitting on maybe ten horses, then phoning while driving back home, spending the next hour and a half on the phone, and staying on it when driving to the races. Luckily Simon McNeill and Carl Llewellyn often drove me to the races, which left me both hands free for dialling!

The day after the appointment was announced I was back in action. Adrian was sitting out the second day of his ban from the King George ride on Barton Bank so I had a chance of closing the gap a little. Not only did I fail to do so, I had one ride which did not exactly lighten my mood.

On the all-weather course at Southwell I rode Doualago for Martin in the selling hurdle. He was warm favourite and made all before quickening away in the straight. He must have been a distance clear when he left his hind legs behind at the last flight and fell. The winner of that race was called It's Not My Fault, but I was not pleased.

Jumping on all-weather surfaces became a very controversial topic a few weeks later and was eventually suspended following an unacceptable level of equine fatalities, but even before that it was never an aspect of the sport with which I felt very comfortable. Of course the existence of all-weather keeps the professionals – including jockeys – active during spells of adverse weather, and it's good to give owners and trainers a wider range of opportunities. But from a jockey's point of view – and from a horse's – the problem is the surface itself. When you fall on either of the all-weather surfaces, there's simply no slide. The horse goes down in front, and rather than slide along as it would do on even firm ground on turf, the back end catches up with the front, which can lead to horrible injuries.

The new hurdles introduced this season were excellent, and I'd like to see them introduced to hurdle races on grass. They're like mini steeplechase fences, and encourage horses to jump better than they do over orthodox hurdles, where they can kick the top bar out and still make half a length. Jumping the new hurdles regularly would make the hurdlers better jumpers of chase fences when they graduate to the bigger obstacles.

The day after Southwell saw Richard at the other all-weather track, for three rides but no winners.

That was Thursday. On Friday Adrian went up to Edinburgh and rode one winner to extend the gap to forty-three, the widest it was all season.

By the Saturday at Warwick the year was eight days old, I'd had fourteen rides and not a single winner. But Martin's horses were beginning to come to themselves again and when I rode a treble for him that day on Prerogative, Honest Word and Gay Ruffian, the deep gloom of the previous weekend seemed a long way away.

After another treble for Martin on the all-weather at Southwell on the Monday and a win on Pridwell at the same track on Tuesday, suddenly the championship did not seem such a remote possibility after all.

As an extra good omen that week I was given a race in which I had actually finished second. My Cup Of Tea had been runner-up to Tina's Lad at Newton Abbot back at the beginning of September, but the winner subsequently failed the dope test, and the official disqualification came through in the first week of January.

On the Friday I flew up to Edinburgh and rode a winner for Brian Rothwell on Lady Blakeney, and then came a highly eventful Saturday at Warwick.

Ascot had been due to stage the Victor Chandler Chase, one of the very best two-mile handicap chases of the season, but when racing was abandoned there the big race was rerouted to Warwick to join what was already a very attractive card featuring the Warwick National, expected to be an informative trial for the Grand National.

I was going to Warwick anyway to ride for Martin, and with the switching of the Victor Chandler came in for a plum spare ride on Viking Flagship for David Nicholson in the big race. The Duke also had Waterloo Boy in the race, whom Adrian had chosen to ride, but I was happy to be on Viking: he'd always been one of my favourite horses when I was with The Duke and I'd won several races on him, including two within the space of three days at the big Punchestown meeting in 1993. He was a very stuffy horse who needed two or three runs to get to peak fitness, but the Victor Chandler was his third of the season – he'd been runner-up in the first two – and I was confident that he'd be straight.

There were four runners in the race and I was familiar with them all – Viking Flagship and Waterloo Boy for The Duke, Egypt Mill Prince, whom I'd ridden for Jenny Pitman and won on at Newbury on Hennessy day, and Billy Bathgate, a good chaser of Nicky Henderson's on which I had also won. So if anyone knew what the outcome of the race should be, I should!

It was desperately wet but Egypt Mill Prince, ridden by Jamie Osborne, took us along at a good gallop, with Adrian and myself settled in behind. At the third last Jamie kicked away and I thought I might be tapped for foot, and when Viking met the second last a little short I found myself with another length to make up. But I knew from riding him that Egypt Mill Prince doesn't find a great deal under pressure, so I kept after him. Viking pinged the last and really battled up the run-in to catch Egypt Mill Prince halfway to the post and win going away by two lengths.

Two races later was the Warwick National, which Adrian

won on Moorcroft Boy for David Nicholson. I rode one of Martin's best chasers, the 1991 Hennessy Gold Cup winner Chatam. This was Chatam's first race since the void Grand National back in April, and he ran extremely well under a large weight to be runner-up, staying on to finish three lengths behind Moorcroft Boy. That was a highly encouraging run, and it was decided that Chatam would be aimed for the 'other' Hennessy, at Leopardstown.

These had been two great races, both containing serious pointers for big races to come. But in terms of the championship duel a far more significant event was the second on the card, the two-and-a-half-mile Westminster Motor-Taxi Insurance Novices' Chase.

I was riding Castle Diamond for Henry Kavanagh and Adrian rode Ramstar for The Duke. I'd never sat on Castle Diamond before, though Henry had asked me to ride him in the past. He'd won at Bangor on the first day of the season, and I'd seen him run a couple of times.

At Warwick he set off well, jumped cleanly, and gave me a grand ride. At the third last Adrian came to challenge me and we were neck and neck over the last two. Ramstar was ahead at the second last but mine jumped the last better, and up the run-in I was always doing just enough to hold on, though Adrian was coming back at me all the way. At the post there was a short head in it.

It had been a driving finish and I was aware that Adrian was being quite hard on Ramstar – I could hear the cracking of the whip on my right, but it certainly didn't sound too bad.

But when we came back into the changing room there was a common view: 'Adrian's going to get hung for that.'

From the stands and on television such a hanging seemed inevitable, especially in the light of the Kempton Park stewards' decision to suspend Adrian after a far less ferocious ride in the King George. Maguire appeared to have given Ramstar two smacks with the whip in his right hand approaching the last fence, then two more just after the last before switching the whip to his left hand and appearing to hit the horse relentlessly all the way to the line – more than twenty times in all, and well beyond the level at which the Jockey Club instructs that stewards look into the matter.

The Warwick stewards duly looked, but to general astonishment it was announced that they had accepted Maguire's explanation that he was waving the whip at the horse and not making contact with him, and that no further action would be taken.

The press hooted with derision at the inconsistency among racecourse stewards. On the Monday morning the Racing Post *took the solemn step of printing an editorial on its front page. Headed 'Time to Sort Out this Mess', it steamed:*

'Saturday should have been a great day for British racing. Instead, it will be remembered as the day the Warwick stewards made the rules a laughing stock . . .

'The three Jockey Club-appointed stewards were just about the only people who did not think Adrian Maguire had broken the whip regulations on Ramstar. Head-to-head with his chief adversary Richard Dunwoody, Maguire was guilty of precisely the sort of frenzied assault on his mount which the Jockey Club guidelines were designed to eliminate.

'He is an outstandingly gifted rider, but on Saturday he broke the rules and should have paid the price. If ever there was a case of improper use of the whip, this was it. Everybody could see that. Except the stewards.'

The halo so recently fitted was already starting to look a little tarnished.

Such was the furore over the apparent inconsistency that the Jockey Club took the unusual step of announcing that it would consider whether its Disciplinary Committee should look into the riding of Ramstar – in other words, that a higher court would decide whether to overturn the verdict of the lower. Meanwhile Richard could at last reflect on a good spell:

After all the problems earlier in the month, that day at Warwick was especially satisfying.

On the Tuesday after the Warwick incident, he rode a double at Folkestone, while on the same course Adrian picked up a four-day ban for careless riding on Spikey, who veered away from the whip on the run-in and interfered with Bollinger. Spikey finished second and Bollinger third behind Mailcom, but the placings were reversed, and Adrian was in hot water again.

It was Richard's thirtieth birthday.

The gap that evening was thirty-one and the champion still faced an uphill struggle, but the black clouds were scudding together to form an umbrella of gloom over the young pretender's prospects, and worse was to come the following day when the Jockey Club confirmed that the Disciplinary Committee would indeed reopen the Ramstar case. The same day Richard rode a double on Pridwell and Doualago on the all-weather at Southwell, and the pendulum of fortune seemed to be swinging his way with a vengeance.

Meanwhile there was that gap to be chipped away at.

Towards the end of January I went up to Haydock – six rides, two winners, one of them Flakey Dove. It was the first time I'd ridden her and she won very easily, beating Charlie Swan on Tiananmen Square by twenty lengths. She gave me a very good feel that day, and I thought at the time that with softish ground at Cheltenham she'd have a great each-way chance in the Champion Hurdle.

I was unlikely to be riding her in the Champion as we were still hopeful that Granville Again would regain his old sparkle, and the day after Haydock it was over to Ireland to ride him in the Irish Champion Hurdle. He ran very disappointingly to come fourth behind Fortune and Fame, ridden by Adrian, and that turned out to be the last time I rode him all season. (I was otherwise occupied when he ran unplaced in the Champion Hurdle, after which he was moved from Martin's to be trained by Len Lungo in Scotland, only to return to Nicholashayne.) He wasn't himself at Leopardstown, and his failure to recapture his form was one of the big disappointments of the season.

A surprise at Leopardstown that Sunday was that I got into trouble with the stewards over my use of the stick after riding Ground War in a handicap hurdle. He was just beaten – half a length – by Frigid Countess, ridden by Larry Hurley, who at nineteen was scoring the second win of his career. We were both severely cautioned, as was Paul Carberry on the third. I must have hit my horse seven or eight times from the last in a very tight finish, but the stewards in Ireland are usually more relaxed about the use of the whip than those in England, so I was a little taken aback. This was after the Jockey Club had announced that Adrian would be up before the Disciplinary Committee over Ramstar, and I thought the Irish may have been trying to tighten up their own rules!

The following week Richard continued to clock up the winners – Raymylette at Leicester on Monday, Devils Den at Chepstow on Tuesday – but the focal point of the week was Adrian's appearance before the Jockey Club Disciplinary Committee on the Thursday to account for his riding of Ramstar at Warwick. He was already serving his four-day ban from the Folkestone incident when he travelled up to London with agent Dave Roberts to face the music.

Adrian left the Portman Square headquarters of the Jockey Club with a six-day ban which meant missing valuable races at Sandown Park and Leopardstown, but he tried to look on the bright side:

'I've learnt a lot being up here today and I'm now going to go away and take a break. I'm only twenty-two, I've still got plenty of time to polish up my riding, come back fresh and ride more winners . . .

'The press built me up to be a superstar and then the next day say I'm the bad boy of racing. I didn't ask to be built up to be a superstar.'

The latter point was picked up by David Nicholson in a letter to the racing papers, referring to 'the irresponsible, sensationalistic and hysterical behaviour of the press'.

A couple of hours after Adrian had been handed his punishment, Richard rode his ninetieth winner of the season, Gales Cavalier at Huntingdon. The gap had now shrunk to twenty-four, and with Adrian facing the prospect of more days off, the title was suddenly up for grabs again. William Hill revised their prices:

Maguire 6–4 on
Dunwoody 11–10

Gales Cavalier was Richard's 998th winner in Britain, and another milestone was round the corner.

Cheltenham on the last Saturday in January started well, with Pridwell winning his first race over hurdles on turf after two races on the all-weather.

Then came Flakey Dove in the Cleeve Hurdle. She had six top-notch opponents – King Credo, Sweet Duke, Mole Board, Triple Witching, Absalom's Lady and Martin Pipe's Sweet Glow, ridden by Martin Foster. Flakey tracked Sweet Duke all the way, then took it up going to the last, stood off and pinged it, and galloped up the hill to win by six lengths.

My thousandth winner. To get there meant a very great deal to me, and I'd had the target in mind for some time. You can't plan where or when it will happen, but to achieve it on a very good horse at Cheltenham was extra special.

Thus Richard became only the fourth jockey in the history of National Hunt racing to reach 1,000 winners in Great Britain. The first was Stan Mellor, who rode 1,035 in a career stretching from 1954 to 1972. His record was passed by John Francome, whose career total came to 1,138 winners between 1970 and 1985, and when Peter Scudamore retired in April 1993 he had registered the highest score of all – 1,678. But Richard had the unique distinction of having ridden the thousand winners and having won the Big Three of jump racing.

If riding the 1,000th winner was a sweet moment, the 1,001st really set Cheltenham on a roar. With Adrian Maguire sitting on the sidelines (this was still the Folkestone ban: the Ramstar holiday was yet to come), David Nicholson asked Richard to ride Waterloo Boy, not only a horse for which the jockey had a particular affection but also one of the most popular jumpers in training.

When he lined up for the Lobb Partnership Hall of Fame Chase, Waterloo Boy had run in forty-four races and won sixteen of them, ridden to fourteen of those victories by Richard (and the other two by Jamie Osborne). But at the age of eleven he was not the force he was in the glory days which saw him as one of the best two-mile chasers in recent memory, and a heroic player in one of the all-time great Cheltenham finishes when in 1990 he and Barnbrook Again, locked together, fought a famous duel from the last in the Queen Mother Champion Chase, Barnbrook Again winning by half a length.

Waterloo Boy had not won for over a year, and the thought had occurred to some that it might be time to retire him: 'That hasn't been discussed yet, but it's obviously in the back of my mind,' wrote David Nicholson in his Racing Post *column on the morning of the race.*

People often ask about how close a jockey gets to the horses he rides. I ride several hundred different horses each season, and with most of them would not expect to have a close relationship at all. Many I'll never have seen, let alone ridden, before they are led into the paddock before the race, but to be able to adapt is simply part of the job.

With most horses I wouldn't expect to have a close relationship, though obviously there are exceptions, and I try to keep in touch with some of my old favourites. West Tip put me on the map and even attended our wedding, along with Charter Party. Very Promising, on whom I won the Mackeson, is still with The Duke, and Desert Orchid still has a very full diary of public engagements.

I'd have to put Waterloo Boy high on any list of horses who

meant a great deal to me. I rode him from his novice hurdle days, and he was always a great favourite in The Duke's yard, and a great favourite of mine. He really puts his head down and tries, and has to be one of the most genuine horses I've ever ridden.

Although Cheltenham is often thought of as his true stamping ground, that January he hadn't won a chase at the course since the Arkle five years before, and that was only his second victory there. (Funnily enough, the runner-up that day, Southern Minstrel, was in the Cheltenham race, and I was offered the ride on him, but I couldn't pass up the chance of riding Waterloo Boy again.)

Waterloo Boy's first Cheltenham win is a slightly embarrassing memory for me. We were upsides Beech Road and Graham McCourt at the last in a three-runner novice chase. The only other runner, Dictalino, had fallen at the fence before, and as we jumped the last I glanced across and saw Beech Road pinging it. So on landing I put my head down and rousted up Waterloo Boy, riding him for all I was worth until we passed the post – only to find that Graham and Beech Road had laid down on landing, and I'd been riding a stirring finish in glorious isolation!

That was the day when Beech Road's fall looked so bad that they put the screens round him, but he was only winded and returned to the course a few months later to win the Champion Hurdle.

As well as that great duel with Barnbrook Again, I rode Waterloo Boy in the Queen Mother Chase three other times. In 1991 we were second to Katabatic, in 1992 third behind Remittance Man (ridden by Jamie Osborne as I'd been claimed by The Duke) and Katabatic, and in 1993 tailed off behind Deep Sensation. Another great memory of the old horse is the race against Norton's Coin in April 1991, over two-and-a-half-miles. Graham McCourt on Norton's Coin and I played cat and mouse with each other all the way round, then went for everything as soon as we'd jumped the last. I've never been so fast up the run-in at Cheltenham, but we were beaten a head.

Those days seemed well behind him when he ran in January, and he was not strongly fancied. He'd never won over two-and-a-half-miles – or two miles five furlongs, as the old Cheltenham two-and-a-half-miles is since they remeasured the course – but he was always going well just off the pace. He didn't get the second last fence quite right, which gave me a bit more work to do, but clawed his way back to join Southern Minstrel and Richville going to the last. He jumped the last brilliantly, then stuck his head down and battled all the way up the hill. He was giving nearly two stone to Richville but he just wouldn't give in as the younger horse pressed him all the way to the line, and at the post won by a head.

This was a particularly great thrill as I wasn't expecting it, and The Duke was ecstatic. It was one of the moments of the season.

Then Brigadier Roscoe Harvey's Relkeel won the last, which added to a memorable day: the Brigadier has long been one of my favourite owners, and to ride another winner for him at Cheltenham was marvellous.

Those four winners brought Richard's tally up to ninety-four. Adrian was on 114, the gap was twenty, and the betting was reheating: Ladbrokes went 6–5 on each of two; William Hill kept Adrian favourite at 11–8 on with Richard at 11–10. 'It's going to be a long old haul,' Richard told the press, 'and I'm going to give it everything I've got.'

Certainly the next week suggested that 'everything I've got' might do the trick. Monday, the last day of January, brought a treble at Plumpton, with Sheer Ability, Habasha and Damier Blanc. Tuesday added one at Nottingham, and Wednesday at Leicester two more: the second of these, Honest Word, was his hundredth winner of the season, marking his fifth successive century. On Thursday Richard switched from the abandoned Towcester to the all-weather track at Lingfield, where he clocked up one more winner in Tel E Thon, not to everyone's approval: Dean Gallagher, who had originally been booked to ride the horse, thought that putting Richard up 'made a mockery' of the system of overnight declaration of jockeys. By such switches, however, championships can be won, and Gallagher himself would be involved in another switch, this time involving Adrian, during the final throes of the season.

Friday was Lingfield again, and a four-timer on the turf track at the same course. The quartet included his only dead heat of the season, on Derrymoss, but the jockeys' title does not deal in half points, and a dead heat counts as much as any thirty-length victory. The last of Richard's winners that day was Lord Relic, in his first run over fences. Starting at 3–1 on, he jumped well and was unextended to win by a distance. The entry in the Dunwoody record book ends: 'smashing prospect'.

Richard had ridden fifteen winners in six racing days, and the gap was down to single figures. Adrian was ahead by just nine.

The next day, Saturday, saw a meeting at Sandown Park which was stacked with high-class races, and with Adrian Maguire now serving his Ramstar ban, Richard came in for some plum spare rides from David Nicholson. Inevitably there was comment in some quarters to the effect that Nicholson should not have been fuelling the title claims of his stable jockey's rival while Adrian was sidelined, but his owners *were entitled to the best available, and if that was Richard Dunwoody, why not? (The same philosophy on occasion led Martin Pipe to put up Adrian when for one reason or another Richard was unavailable, including on two runners at the Cheltenham Festival.)*

Since moving to Martin's I'd stayed on very good terms with The Duke and have always got on well with his owners. Two of my three winners at Sandown that day, after I'd won the first on Devils Den for Martin, were on David's horses.

Baydon Star beat Crystal Spirit convincingly in the Scilly Isles Novices Chase, then Second Schedual won the Agfa Diamond Chase from a top-class field – Zeta's Lad, Young Hustler, Bradbury Star and King's Curate, ridden for Martin by Mark Perrett. My final mount for The Duke was Wonder Man, who went down by a neck to Storm Alert in the two-mile chase.

Two other encouraging rides on Pipe horses that afternoon were on Olympian, third on his seasonal reappearance in the big handicap hurdle ('needed it, good run', reads the Dunwoody ledger) and Valfinet, second to Muse in the Agfa Hurdle ('lovely horse, make a chaser').

Adrian returned to the saddle on the Monday with the score 114–108 in his favour but with the bookmakers shortening Richard to around 2–1 on.

'I've been taking a close look at my style and have concentrated on keeping my whip low,' Adrian was quoted as saying on the morning of his return, but perhaps he had not been taking a close enough look at the course plan of Fontwell Park. Riding at the Sussex track on his first day back, he rode a finish in a handicap hurdle a circuit too early and pulled up his mount, Access Sun. He was fined £400.

Richard, meanwhile, was continuing to ride winners, including Nicky Henderson's Raymylette at Warwick.

Raymylette was a horse that we thought might be a little chancy in his jumping, so Yogi Breisner was brought in to school him. Yogi, who's had a lot of experience with eventers as well as racehorses, does amazing things teaching horses to jump – loose schooling, then with riders over doubles and trebles, and it's extraordinary how he can get a horse which had jumped little more than a hurdle to take on four-foot parallels. He just has this knack of getting a horse's confidence.

Raymylette went on to win the Cathcart Challenge Cup at the Cheltenham National Hunt Festival. Meanwhile, smaller fish were tasting sweet:

That week I also had a couple at Wincanton for Martin, and on the Saturday didn't go to Newbury for the Tote Gold Trophy – what used to be and is still widely referred to as the Schweppes – but instead went up to Uttoxeter. It was well worth it, as I had four winners: Honest Word for Martin, Sheer Ability (again) for Charlie Mann, Nakir – who went on to win the Arkle Chase at the Festival – for Simon Christian, and Corner Boy for The Duke.

Then on the Sunday it was over to Leopardstown again, but it was a disappointing trip. Chatam ran limply to finish fourth behind Jodami in the Hennessy Gold Cup, Chirkpar was a distant third behind Jim Dreaper's highly promising prospect Merry Gale, and my other two rides were both unplaced.

Racing on the Monday and Tuesday was abandoned, then I had a double on the all-weather at Southwell on the Wednesday, and then, after a few other cancelled meetings, a good double at Wincanton's best pre-Cheltenham fixture on 23 February with Valfinet in the Kingwell Hurdle and Thumbs Up, a horse of huge promise with a high cruising speed, in the novice chase.

Kempton Park's late February meeting is always full of clues for Cheltenham, and I started well with a double on the Friday – Honest Word and Cloghlans Bay (who sadly died later in the year), both for Martin.

The Saturday of that Kempton fixture is one of the best days' jumping of the whole year, and I had some highly promising rides lined up. Balasani won the Rendlesham Hurdle from Cab On Target, a race I really enjoyed: he showed a terrific turn of foot in the straight and won by five lengths despite missing the last. Rough Quest, favourite for the Racing Post Chase, fell at the last: he was in contention but getting tired, and just lay down on landing. And the saddest disappointment was Lord Relic, who fell two out and injured himself, behind Monsieur Le Cure.

But there was one wonderful performance that day which put it up among the highlights of the season – and not only for me.

Remittance Man had not run for fifteen months, having injured a tendon at Huntingdon in November 1992, and his reappearance was very keenly awaited by the racing public, by his trainer Nicky Henderson, and not least by myself.

It is not always easy to explain the particular feel of individual horses. With Desert Orchid, my first and lasting impression was of sheer power and strength. He had a tremendously strong neck and front, and everything you did on him was a matter of channelling that power. With Remittance Man the key is athleticism. He had been a reasonably good but by no means brilliant hurdler, and it took him quite a long time to lose his novice tag. But the first time I schooled him over fences, on

Lambourn's Mandown gallop, he felt as if he was on springs. He was extraordinarily athletic, but this had never been allowed full expression when he was racing over hurdles. So we were very hopeful that he would make an exceptional chaser, and I flew back from America especially to ride him in his first novice chase at Leicester in November 1990. We were not disappointed.

He's always been a joy to ride. Riding any chaser the jockey must help the horse, give it confidence so that you are working together as a close-knit team, and with Remittance Man this simply came naturally. Horses like him help you see a stride, and give you the confidence and assurance to ask them to go for a long one.

But at the age of ten he was getting on a bit, and it was asking a great deal to expect him to be as good as ever at Kempton after such a long layoff. He's quite a light horse, and it was easier to get him fit first time out than some other horses, but we didn't expect him to be race sharp, and the opposition in the Emblem Chase was extremely stiff – only three opponents, but they were Deep Sensation, the reigning two-mile champion, Wonder Man (ridden by Adrian), and Richard Lee's good chaser Space Fair.

Remittance Man jumped beautifully and tracked the leaders down the back straight, but the crunch time was always going to be when lack of race fitness started to tell after turning for home. Deep Sensation led us before the second last but I still had plenty of horse under me, and the old boy jumped into the lead at the last and went away from Deep Sensation without my needing to put him under serious pressure.

It was a tremendous performance, and we got a great reception from the crowd when we returned to the unsaddling enclosure. Racing always needs its equine stars, and jumping fans stay deeply loyal to their old favourites. They just loved seeing Remittance Man back to his best – all being well, it was next stop Cheltenham.

The Kempton meeting is in effect the last of the big pre-Cheltenham fixtures, and the next three weeks or so are taken up with assessing the prospects for all the major races at jumping's greatest meeting in the middle of March. Fine tuning of riding arrangements was to come, but with Remittance Man rehabilitated and the Martin Pipe string having shaken off whatever was affecting it in the darker months of the winter, Richard could look forward to an exciting and successful Festival.

First, though, there was bread and butter to be earned and that gap to be further compressed. On the Monday after Kempton, the last day of February, he won the first at Plumpton on Strong Case, but the day had its disappointing angle:

Whitechapel was my one attempt in the season to ride a winner for Her Majesty Queen Elizabeth the Queen Mother and help her towards the total of four hundred winners as an owner, which she finally achieved in May. He was odds-on favourite and I was very optimistic that he would give me my first winner in the Queen Mother's colours – I've ridden a few for her over the years, but never with any great success. Sadly, Whitechapel was beaten three and a half lengths by Isaiah.

That was a disappointment, and the same day brought another with the announcement that Carvill's Hill would not run again. A recurrence of leg injury had ruled out any comeback, and thereby finished any chance of Richard's getting to ride him.

He had never sat on the horse, but none the less had a special place for him in his own racing memories:

The performance which Carvill's Hill put up when he won the Welsh National in December 1991 was without doubt the finest of any horse in a race in which I took part. He was just sensational. I rode another of Martin Pipe's runners that day, Aquilifer, but like everything else in the race we were soon struggling as Scu on Carvill's Hill built up a gigantic lead. I'd never been so fast in a three-mile-six-furlong chase, and coming down the straight towards the end of the first circuit called across to Neale Doughty on Twin Oaks that Scu must have thought he was in a two-mile chase! Scu knew exactly what he was doing, of course, and powered on. Poor Aquilifer, who was a very good horse, was legless at least a mile out, but plugged on to finish third, a short head behind Party Politics but twenty lengths adrift of Carvill's. Not even Desert Orchid at his peak matched Carvill's Hill that day.

So one pre-season dream was not to come true, but on every other front things were decidedly looking up. By the end of racing on 28 February the gap was down to a mere four winners, Richard was firmly re-established as odds-on favourite to resume his place at the top of the tree, and a highly successful Cheltenham Festival was just coming into sight.

What could possibly go wrong now?

6

FLASHPOINT

The Junior Selling Hurdle for four-year-olds, the first race of a modest Nottingham card on Tuesday 1 March, two weeks before the opening day of the Cheltenham National Hunt Festival, looked an unlikely candidate for the pivotal race of Richard Dunwoody's season. Over two miles of Nottingham's left-handed circuit, the race had added prize money of just £2,250 – the minimum for a hurdle race – and only two of the thirteen runners had won a race over jumps.

Richard's mount Raggerty, trained by Steve Coathup, had won three but had the reputation of being an unreliable performer, while Mr Geneaology, trained by John White, had won six of his ten starts over hurdles and back in July had given

Adrian Maguire his second winner of the season at the opening fixture at Bangor-on-Dee. Adrian was in the saddle again at Nottingham, and Mr Geneaology went off the hot favourite at 5–4 on. Raggerty was third choice at 5–1.

This nondescript race was to become the flashpoint of the duel for the championship.

I'd never ridden Raggerty before. I'd seen him run a couple of times and had read him up in the form book, so I had an idea that he may hang. But he'd shown decent form for a seller, and other than Mr Geneaology he was certainly the horse to be riding in the race.

Steve Coathup told me to have him handy, then keep firing away from the third last: he should keep going. Raggerty had form where he'd been struggling early on in his races but had plugged on towards the end, and I was hopeful that we could take the sting out of Mr Geneaology up the long home straight.

I bounced out from the start with the idea of keeping him up with the pace and on the bridle, and all the way was able to lay up near the leaders.

Going into the far bend I was one horse off the rail, with Willie McFarland on Manon Lescaut, at 20–1 much the less fancied of John White's two runners, on my inside. I could hear Adrian just behind, shouting to Willie for light. But to give Adrian light on the inner, Willie had to carry me wider round that bottom bend. Naturally I took a little bit of an aversion to this, and was not inclined to lose my position. So I was trying to keep Willie in, Adrian was trying to push him out, and Manon Lescaut got sandwiched between us and dropped out very quickly.

Rounding the turn into the straight, with three hurdles to jump and a couple of horses in front of me, I was still one off the inside rail. Then I pushed Raggerty into the lead going into the third last, and at that hurdle actually jumped the inside flight, next to the wing, so I assumed that the inner was my right of way.

Adrian was my chief danger and I looked across for him – to my right, assuming he would have pulled out to challenge up the centre of the track. I heard horses coming up the outside and assumed that he'd be in that group, and as I looked across my horse went slightly right-handed, drifting off the inner. No Adrian on my right, so I glanced across to my left – and there he was, ready to deliver his challenge.

There is a rule in race riding – though not one to be found in any official rule book – about coming up another jockey's inside. Whether it is a seven-pound claiming conditional jockey challenging the reigning champion or the other way round – or, as in this case, the champion and the heir presumptive – it is simply not done, unless the move can be executed quickly and smoothly. Get it right and you steal the advantage, and possibly the race. Get it wrong and either antagonist can end up with an unanticipated holiday, as Peter Scudamore and Bruce Dowling discovered after a barging match at Newbury's cross hurdle in 1988 – three weeks' suspension for each of them.

If you're going to go up someone's inside, you have to do it quickly. I learnt that very early on in my career, one day at Huntingdon when I tried to go down John Francome's inner in a novice hurdle. I thought I had a bit of poke but I didn't, and when I asked my horse to slip past he couldn't go through with it. I nearly ended up jumping the open ditch that day! The trouble starts when you gauge wrongly how much you've got under the bonnet.

Adrian had got into a barging match with Mick Fitzgerald at Ludlow a few days before the Nottingham race, going up Mick's inner and nearly getting himself knocked out the side door in the process. He won that race.

At Nottingham, I knew well enough what he was up to. There was not a running rail along the whole extent of the hurdle course, and the hurdles that day were placed closer than usual to the chase track on the inner than they usually are, on account of the bad ground. I thought Adrian had strayed onto the chase track and was going up a place he shouldn't have been, and I felt it was quite legitimate to go across to stop him.

We connected, but Adrian kept on trying to get inside me before we jumped the second last. I wasn't going to let him do that, and the second time I eased Raggerty over to him we certainly made contact. Of course I didn't mean to run him out, but at the same time I was saying: You're not going to go down the inside, you can come out and round me, but you're not going to take me up my inner. Mr Geneaology had enough light, but not the nerve to go through with Adrian's move, so he ran out. I heard the crash of the rails as he went through them but I didn't look round. The horse had run out. We get run out. We've got to look after ourselves at the same time.

Mr Geneaology had crashed into the running rail leading up to the second last flight of hurdles and swerved violently out of the race, Adrian Maguire just managing to stay aboard. Left clear, Raggerty hit the last flight but reached the winning post fifteen lengths ahead of the second favourite Ho-Joe.

My immediate reaction as I pulled up was that this was something that would no doubt be looked at by the stewards, but that I was in the right. Adrian had been going somewhere that he shouldn't have been going.

Steve Coathup was quite sure in his own mind that we

wouldn't have any trouble, but we were soon to find ourselves in the minority.

I went back to the changing room, where I watched the replay on the television screen with Norman Williamson, who turned to me and said: 'I think you'll be in a bit of trouble.' Then Jonjo O'Neill came up. He hadn't seen the incident but offered the advice: 'If I were you I'd just pretend you hadn't seen he was there.' That would have been quite difficult to get away with, as it would be quite plain from the recording of the race that I'd looked across at him!

Adrian himself said nothing.

We were starting to change into our colours for our next ride when the stewards' secretary Geoffrey Forster came in to say that they'd like to see us both in the Stewards' Room.

While waiting to go in, like naughty schoolboys outside the headmaster's study, I sat on the bench outside the stewards' room and Adrian – clearly none too happy with affairs – stood. Still he had said nothing to me about what had happened. I'd heard that Mr Geneaology's trainer John White was furious about the incident, but I hadn't encountered him since the race.

Rule 153 in the Rules of Racing concerns riding offences, and the Jockey Club's Instruction H12 defines the different categories of illegal riding – reckless riding, intentionally causing interference, irresponsible riding, careless riding and improper riding. In the case of Raggerty and Mr Geneaology, it seemed to be a matter of whether the offence would be that of intentionally causing interference ('A rider is guilty of intentionally causing interference if he purposely interferes with any other horse or rider') or careless riding ('A rider is guilty of careless riding if he fails to take reasonable steps to avoid causing interference or causes interference by misjudgment, or inattention').

We were called in. Adrian gave his evidence first. When I heard the Stewards' Secretary assure Adrian that he had every right to go where he did, I feared the worst. The questioning carried on along those lines – that Adrian had plenty of room and I'd come across. I said my horse was a hard ride – he was cited in Timeform as difficult – and that he'd hung right with me and then gone left with me: it wasn't my fault but the horse's doing. I suppose you'd have to call these defences white lies! We looked at the film of the head-on and side-on views of the incident, but not the scout – the camera which films the runners from behind – and when I saw that film I realized I didn't have very much defence.

My aim from then on was to try to get it classed as careless riding, which would have been at worst a four-day penalty, rather than reckless or intentional. Then we were told to go out of the stewards' room. The next race was coming up, which I wasn't riding in, so they held the inquiry over until after that. We were called back in to be given the verdict – which was that I was guilty of intentionally causing interference, and my horse was disqualified.

I was given fourteen days' suspension, to commence nine days later. Cheltenham was out.

Still Adrian had made no comment directly to me, but a couple of races later when we were on the preliminary scales together, he said: 'I'm very sorry you're going to miss Cheltenham.'

I was sorry too. I was gutted, but what was the point in dwelling on it? I had to make something positive out of a very negative happening, so decided straight away that if I didn't appeal – and watching the replay later that evening suggested an appeal would not be worth while – I would take a break, and get clean away during Cheltenham week.

On the way home from Nottingham several of the jockeys – including myself and Adrian, who had one winner later in the afternoon – met up at a TGI Fridays restaurant on the outskirts of Coventry. I was pretty aggravated about what had happened, but bought Adrian a drink, with the suggestion – slightly tongue in cheek: 'You'll think twice about going there again!'

For the press, the incident was the biggest story to come out of jump racing since the void Grand National the previous April, and was almost too good to be true – champion facing the loss of his crown barges young upstart out of the race, needle, grudge match, etc. Coverage was not marked by any measure of sympathy for Richard, a view shared by John White, trainer of Mr Geneaology, whose view of Richard was blunt: 'He deserves what he got.'

Tabloid headline writers went to town –

'DUN-BADDY' (Today)
'DUN FOR!' (Sun)
'DUNRIDING!' (Daily Star)

– and the stories beneath those headlines played up the theme of arch-rivalry. The Sun *spoke of a 'grudge battle'. Today called it 'title suicide' and described how 'the bitter battle for the jump jockeys' championship turned nasty yesterday'. The* Daily Express *called the incident 'a mad moment', the* Guardian *lamented how Richard's 'split second's aberration would seem to have ruined all the hard work he had put into clawing back Maguire', and in the* Daily Telegraph *J. A. McGrath pondered:*

'In the calm of morning, one could well sit and wonder why a jockey such as the talented Dunwoody apparently throws all caution to the wind and jeopardises his chances of competing at the single most important race meeting of the entire National Hunt season . . .

'There has been needle between Dunwoody and Maguire this season – nothing noticeable, but it has been there – and it only takes an incident such as at Nottingham to spark a blaze of irrationality that a rider may later regret.'

In his column in the Daily Mail, Peter Scudamore, who had been involved in more 'up-the-inner' incidents than all the rest of the commenting journalists put together, brought the expertise of the practitioner to bear:

'Personal experience allows me to understand the anguish Dunwoody will be feeling this morning as he surveys the wreckage of a season that has suddenly crash-landed . . .

'As a professional jump jockey you have gone out and tried to do your best for owner, trainer and punters and you are made to feel like a criminal . . .

'Maguire broke one of the unwritten rules of race-riding – never try to steal ground up the inside. It is something you learn, and inherit from older colleagues, as a young rider . . .

'The official rule book in the uncompromising world of jump racing is, on occasions, superseded by the etiquette of the weighing room.'

The amount of money which Richard might forfeit through missing Cheltenham was laboriously calculated in several papers, and his own post-inquiry comment – 'I suppose it has not come at a very good time of the season' – widely quoted, often with an expression of surprise at its mildness.

Rivalry between Dunwoody and Maguire even made a curious little column named 'Feuds Corner' in the following weekend's Sunday Times: 'In four seconds of equine dodgems, between 2.25.49 p.m. and 2.25.52 p.m. last Tuesday, Dunwoody said sayonara to a second title. The personality contrast reinforces this classic grudge match between rising star and fading champ.'

The notion that the incident had at a stroke cost Richard the championship was widespread, and reflected in the bookmakers' new prices on the title. As Richard resolutely reduced the deficit during the second half of February he was 15–8 on favourite in William Hill's book, Adrian 11–8 against. By three-thirty on the afternoon of 1 March they had flip-flopped yet again, to 5–2 on Maguire, 7–4 against Dunwoody.

Unlike its fellow tabloids, the Daily Mirror *resisted the temptation to dun any more puns from the jockey's name and opted for a mere 'BANNED', but had the scoop the following day with Richard's own account, told to the* Mirror *racing correspondent Charlie Fawcus:*

'Guilty – that was me at Nottingham on Tuesday and that's why I'm not going to appeal against the fourteen–day ban the stewards there gave me for doing a Vinny Jones job on Adrian Maguire.

'I made a mistake and I'm going to pay for it. I pushed Adrian out, but I wasn't trying to kill my pal as some people are trying to make out – the idea that we are out to get one another is just ridiculous.'

The following day the press circus crowded into Fontwell Park to get 'best of friends' photographs as the two jockeys emerged from the weighing room, and by the end of the week things had started to return to normal.

Richard paid another visit to sports psychologist Peter Terry: 'Richard had seemed to write off the championship, but I tried to convince him that every cloud has a silver lining: he could take a holiday, recharge the batteries and use the break to improve his mood. As for the Nottingham incident itself, it seemed a case of six of one and half a dozen of the other – Adrian trying to take liberties and Richard defending what he considered to be his rightful position.'

There were a few more days' riding before the ban began. I had one winner on the Wednesday – the highly promising chaser All For Luck for Martin at Fontwell – and a couple on the Thursday at Warwick before driving up to Ludlow to ride Cyborgo for Martin in the last there. He started odds-on but was beaten into second by Nicky Henderson's Golden Spinner, a horse I'd ridden regularly.

Friday was one winner at Lingfield – Sheer Ability yet again – and a very disappointing run from Martin's Triumph Hurdle hope General Mouktar, beaten twenty lengths.

Ironically, on the approach to the enforced break which appeared catastrophic in terms of his title chances, Richard had been whittling away at the deficit, which by the Saturday morning stood at just four. With seven rides at Newbury, there seemed every prospect of a further reduction in the gap that afternoon, though Adrian had fancied mounts at Stratford.

Richard's second ride at Newbury brought his first winner of the day in the shape of Flakey Dove, who won the Berkshire Hurdle by twenty lengths without her jockey having to put her under any apparent pressure.

In the next race Richard sat for only the second time ever on one of the most interesting inmates of Martin Pipe's yard, Miinnehoma. Owned by comedian Freddie Starr (who had selected and bought the horse himself at the Doncaster Sales in 1988, when he reputedly registered his bids by sticking out his tongue), Miinnehoma had advertised his immense promise when beating Bradbury Star in the Sun Alliance Chase at Cheltenham in 1992, but had been plagued with problems since and by the day of the Newbury race had not run for 399 days. 'He will need the race,' Martin Pipe informed the press, stressing that the horse's main aim was the Cheltenham Gold Cup, possibly followed by the Grand National.

I'd only sat on Miinnehoma once before that race, when I schooled him at Martin's. He jumped very well then, but after such a long layoff we really didn't know what to expect.

They were in for a pleasant surprise, as Miinnehoma showed much of his old fire to take the lead up the straight, only to lose it to Forest Sun going to the last. But on touching down he rallied, and passed Forest Sun on the run-in to win going away. His future looked bright, as did that of Richard's third winner of the afternoon, All For Luck.

Meanwhile at Stratford, Adrian rode a single winner, to bring the gap to two, the closest it had been since the first week of the season. But enforced idleness for the champion was looming.

I went to Leopardstown on the Sunday – five rides, no winners – then had a quiet three days at Windsor, Sedgefield and Folkestone: thirteen rides, no winners.

The ban started on the Thursday. I spent the first couple of days catching up on office work, then flew out with a friend to Val d'Isère for a week's skiing. (Carol, who would be photographing at Cheltenham, remained at home.)

While out there, I kept trying to concentrate on the bright side of the situation, and so didn't go to great lengths to find out what was happening at the Festival – there's nothing positive in worrying about what's going to win and what's not going to win. I saw the first day's main results – Flakey Dove in the Champion Hurdle, Arctic Kinsman in the opener, Nakir in the Arkle – in Wednesday's *Paris-Turf*. Thursday they had the result of the Champion Chase and Danoli in the Sun Alliance, and on the last day The Fellow was of course on the front page. The one Martin Pipe winner I missed was Balasani, and I didn't know that he'd won until the Saturday, when some lads and girls from the Royal Agricultural College at Cirencester came out, and they let me know what had won throughout the week. I have to confess, though, that I woke very early Friday morning in Val d'Isère wondering if Miinnehoma had won the Gold Cup . . .

He need not have worried. Miinnehoma had not won the Gold Cup, and of the horses which Richard might have expected to have ridden at Cheltenham but for the suspension, only Balasani won – and that was on the disqualification of Avro Anson in the BonusPrint Stayers' Hurdle.

Ridden by Mick Fitzgerald, Remittance Man – who would probably have been the banker bet for Dunwoody followers at the Festival – made an uncharacteristic misjudgement when putting down at the third last fence in the Queen Mother Champion Chase and fell. Granville Again was a distant seventh in the Smurfit Champion Hurdle behind Flakey Dove (whom Richard would not have been likely to ride unless Granville Again had not run). Martin Pipe had four runners in the Daily Express Triumph Hurdle: Richard would probably have ridden Pridwell, who ran well to finish seventh, or Devils Den, twelfth.

And Miinnehoma? He was ridden in the Tote Gold Cup by none other than Adrian Maguire. Had the challenger won the season's premier chase on one of the Dunwoody rides, that might have tested Richard's determination to look on the positive side of his ban, but after looking to hold a chance approaching the second last, Miinnehoma weakened to finish seventh behind The Fellow.

Adrian himself rode two winners at the Festival, both for David Nicholson: Viking Flagship won the Queen Mother

Mud, mud, glorious mud: after riding Sesame Seed in the novices' hurdle on the Friday of the Aintree Grand National meeting. Note the three pairs of Uvex goggles, which certainly did the trick that day. *Mercury Press Agency/Philip Coppell*

The moment the Martell Grand National nearly slipped away: Miinnehoma at second Becher's. *Gerry Cranham/Paul Cranham*

.Just after the last fence: the riderless Young Hustler leads Adrian on Moorcroft Boy, as Miinnehoma and I bide our time...
Carol Dunwoody

.... and pass the post clear of Just So and Simon Burrough.
Trevor Jones

Catching up with Freddie
Starr after the National,
courtesy of Martin Pipe's
mobile phone, with Desmond
Lynam trying to bug the
conversation. *Colin Turner*

Definitely one for the judge: Boscean Chieftain (no. 4) just holds off Crystal Spirit at Cheltenham in April. *Racecourse Technical Services*

Taking a bank at Punchestown in the La Touche Cup on Leagaune upsides Tony 'Harvey' Martin on Tasse du Thé. *Liam Healy*

Pat Eddery, eat your heart out! Putting on the flat-race style in the bumper at Chepstow in May on Distant Echo, owned by Carol's boss Mel Fordham. *Carol Dunwoody*

In front at last: Merlins Wish at Bangor on 14 May puts me one ahead of Adrian in the championship race. *Colin Turner*

The duellists. *Mail on Sunday/James Bareham*

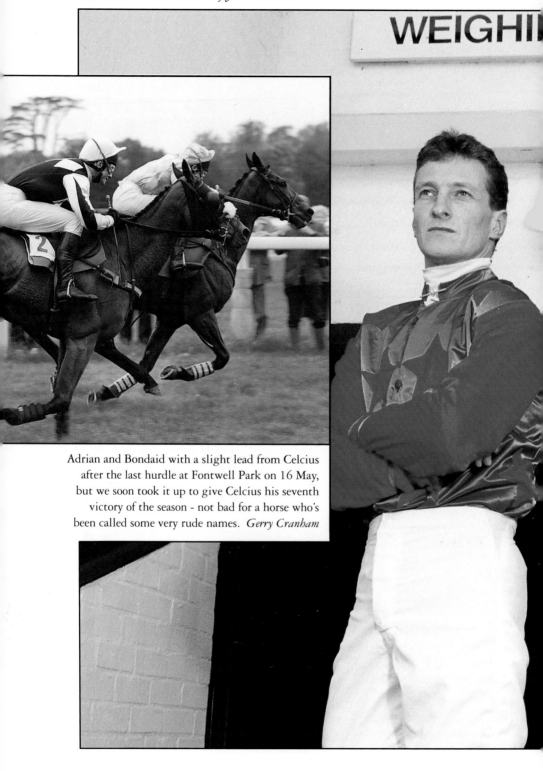

WEIGHI

Adrian and Bondaid with a slight lead from Celcius after the last hurdle at Fontwell Park on 16 May, but we soon took it up to give Celcius his seventh victory of the season - not bad for a horse who's been called some very rude names. *Gerry Cranham*

ROOM

States of undress: in the changing room at Stratford on the penultimate day of the season with Graham McCourt (I think that Coke is there for show!) and Adrian. Anyone wanting the name of my hairdresser, please get in touch. *Les Hurley*

The final day: Adrian and I with our valets, Pat Taylor (left) and John Buckingham, at Stratford before Errant Knight's race... *Les Hurley*

... and after it with winning owner Mrs Sheila Cartridge. *Les Hurley*

The end. At Market Rasen on 4 June, with the championship finally won, I'm given a lift by Graham Bradley (left) and Terry Kent, while Martin Brennan and Norman Williamson perform a similar service for Adrian. *Kenneth Bright*

Champion Chase after a superb Maguire ride in a pulsating finish with Travado and Deep Sensation, and Mysilv sprinted up the hill to win the Daily Express Triumph Hurdle.

While these great events were being played out, Richard was on the slopes in Val d'Isère reflecting on how the Nottingham disaster might yet be turned to his advantage, and putting into practice Peter Terry's exhortation to think positively.

The ban caused an unexpected holiday, but it proved a blessing in disguise. With no big freeze-up over the last few winters, and with all-weather racing filling in the unscheduled short gaps, we haven't had the chance for the occasional five or six days off, and you do need that chance to recharge the batteries.

If a jockey is riding flat out all season it's impossible to keep up the same level of concentration in the later months as in the earlier, without a break. You get spates of falls – I did at Christmas time – and one reason is that it's so hard to keep up concentration. Obviously there are one or two that are going to fall anyway, but equally there are one or two that fall that shouldn't. If you're not fresh, it's very hard to keep concentrating on the job in hand.

The worst thing about missing the Cheltenham Festival was not so much the financial side of it – though the press had made much of what I might have earned with a full book of rides there and a couple of big winners – but the actual competing. The atmosphere and the thrill of Cheltenham are incomparable. All jump jockeys look forward to the meeting from the earliest part of the season, and once Christmas and the King George are behind you, Cheltenham dominates your thoughts.

It's the same whether you've won some of the big races there or whether that first major Festival victory remains a burning ambition. Soon after my suspension came a very controversial ban on Norman Williamson at Doncaster, which caused him, like me, to miss Cheltenham – in his case costing him a Champion Hurdle on Flakey Dove. When I saw that result in the *Paris-Turf* out in Val d'Isère I felt desperately sorry for him. Those winners in the big races at Cheltenham mean so much: you'd give your right hand to win a Champion Hurdle.

The Raggerty/Mr Geneaology incident seemed to have cost Richard dear as far as the championship was concerned. When he bought Adrian that famous drink on the way back from Nottingham the score between them was 129 to 124, a gap of five. After reducing the gap to two the following weekend, Richard saw Adrian increase it again, and when he pulled off his riding boots after partnering Pond House in a National Hunt Flat race at Folkestone on 9 March he was on 131 to Adrian's 138, a deficit of seven.

By the time he pulled those boots on again before going out to ride the 100–1 chance Amys Delight in a novice hurdle at Wincanton on 24 March, Richard was still on 131, but Adrian Maguire had taken advantage of his rival's absence to push his own score up to 156. The gap was now twenty-five.

7

COMING BACK

The day before Richard's return to the saddle, Adrian had struck a hefty blow for his own corner with a four-timer at Worcester, a blow for Richard compounded by two of those winners coming from rides which would normally have been his own: Charlie Mann's Sheer Ability, on whom he had already won five times this season, and Ron Hodges' Starlap.

And when Richard did finally get back into action at Wincanton, he did not exactly land running.

Amys Delight pulled up in the opener, then I got unseated from Nos Na Gaoithe three from home in the next. My ride in the third was Lexy Lady, which I pulled up after she got tailed off, and then I pulled up Honeybeer Mead in the fourth. Four rides, and I hadn't even got round! Cheerful Times at least completed the course in the fifth and looked certain to win before we were caught in the last couple of strides by Jamie Osborne on Front Street and beaten a short head.

I found myself wishing I was still out on the ski slopes.

Then Boscean Chieftain, on his début over fences, won the novices' chase by twenty lengths despite hitting the last and the outlook didn't seem so bad.

The bandwagon was rolling again. Two winners at Ludlow on Friday put Richard up to 134 for the season, and as Adrian had not scored since Richard's return, that brought the gap back to twenty-two. The official Dunwoody line when fending off relentless press enquiries about his mood and his prospects following his layoff was that he was determined to give it his best shot, but for all the publicly expressed optimism, he knew perfectly well that twenty-two winners adrift and little more than ten weeks of the season to go meant a mountain to climb.

But that peak seemed significantly nearer by the Saturday night after a memorable afternoon at Newbury.

Adrian was hurt after a fall in the first – which I won on Daring Past – and gave up the rest of his rides for the afternoon. I won two more on Destiny Calls and All For Luck, then Toby Balding asked me to ride one of his which Adrian was due to be on, Senior Steward, and that spare gave me my fourth winner of the day.

The gap, twenty-five on the morning of Richard's return, was now eighteen.

The next scheduled race meeting was at Newton Abbot on Monday, but before that Richard had a busy weekend.

Sunday afternoon he travelled up to London to take part in
A Question of Sport, the hugely popular television sports quiz
hosted by David Coleman and played between teams captained
by former England rugby captain Bill Beaumont and cricketer
Ian Botham. Richard was in Bill Beaumont's team with England
soccer captain Tony Adams against Roger Black and Nigel
Walker with Ian Botham. Richard's team lost, but it was the per-
fect run-up to one of the big social occasions of a jockey's year.

The 1993 Jockeys' Association of Great Britain annual awards
– predictably nicknamed 'The Lesters' – were given out at a
lavish dinner and ceremony at the Kensington Hilton Hotel in
London, and the Maguire–Dunwoody rivalry was very much in
evidence: Adrian was named Jockey of the Year, and Richard,
for the third time, Jump Jockey of the Year.

Compère Richard Pitman paid tribute to Richard's stamina:
'He can go on until five a.m. and drink with his friends from the
Metropolitan Police' – alluding to a little local difficulty after
the awards dinner a year earlier which found the soon-to-be
champion jockey banged up in a cell in Paddington Green police
station after a late-nightlearly-morning misunderstanding. The
incident had instantly become a humanizing seam in the opaque
fabric of the Dunwoody persona: when he lets his hair down, he
lets it down long.

This year I managed to stay well clear of the long arm of the
law, though the next day at Newton Abbot there were a few
sore heads. A group of us stayed at the Hilton and drove
straight down to the races on the Monday. Most of us were
feeling a little tired and under the weather, and a Worst Turned
Out Jockey Award was invented – or rather, a prize for the rider
who looked the worst for wear. It was a photo-finish between a
West Country representative and one from Lambourn.

I had three more winners that day at Newton Abbot, including taking the novice chase on Crosula, who must represent the training performance of the season for Martin Pipe. He had been pulled up in his previous two races and fallen in the one before that, and had only ever finished in front of five horses in his life. Martin had had him in the yard for just five weeks and had put a tremendous amount of effort into schooling him, and for him to come out and win as he did that day was a great tribute to all the lads in the yard who had brought him along.

Celcius for Martin and Blue Doctor for Ron Hodges were my other winners, but Adrian had passed the doctor after his Newbury fall and got one back.

That left the gap at sixteen – already nine fewer than just before Richard's return.

If he was on a roll, the momentum was kept up the following day at Sandown Park with Martha's Son, a winner for his old mentor Tim Forster, and it sparked a memory of riding for The Captain at the same meeting the previous year after his altercation with the constabulary.

When I handed The Captain my saddle before the race he said: 'I always thought you were a jockey who went to bed with a glass of milk and a pile of videos to improve your riding. If I'd known you went round getting yourself locked up I'd never have employed you.'

With the Grand National less than two weeks away and the pulse of the sport perceptibly quickening after the post-Cheltenham lull, a good card at Ascot on the Wednesday offered more evidence that the scales of fortune were tipping towards Richard and away from his rival.

Adrian had a bad fall in the opener when Coiled Spring broke his neck, and he gave up his remaining five rides of the afternoon. I won the big staying hurdle on Sweet Glow for Martin, beating Avro Anson a head after a great battle from the last, and then had a double when picking up one of Adrian's – High Baron for Robert Alner.

Adrian was temporarily sidelined with the gap down to fourteen, and in the betting the pair flip-flopped yet again. From 6–4 on Maguire, 11–10 Dunwoody, William Hill now went 11–8 on Dunwoody, evens Maguire.

The same day at Ascot, Richard's great friend and travelling companion Carl Llewellyn broke his leg in a freak accident. While circling at the start on Ghia Gneuiagh, he was kicked by another of the runners – Hops And Pops, who went on to win the race. It looked as if the Grand National ride on the well-fancied Young Hustler was out for Llewellyn, illustrating yet again the capricious part that fate plays in a jump jockey's life.

So ended Richard Dunwoody's March. It had promised great deeds at Cheltenham then turned sour beyond belief on its very first day and given him an unanticipated skiing holiday in the sun at Val d'Isère. Now it closed with him rapidly clawing back his rival's lead. One way and another, it had been quite a month.

April held the prospect of the Grand National early and the Whitbread Gold Cup late, but began on a humbler stage: Newton Abbot on Easter Saturday.

I had three winners on the Saturday and one on Easter Monday, while Adrian also had one at Newton Abbot on the Monday to leave the gap at twelve.

Then on the Wednesday I won on Couldn't Be Better for

Charlie Brooks at Ascot, which set me up nicely for the Grand National meeting at Aintree.

The National meeting is second only to Cheltenham and comparable with Punchestown as a great festival of jump racing. I had rides in all seven races on the first day, and my one winner was one of the great thrills of the season – Docklands Express.

Now twelve years old, Docklands had been a great servant to Kim Bailey's yard for years: he won the Whitbread in 1991 after that controversial finish with Cahervillahow, he'd run a close third to Cool Ground in the 1992 Gold Cup, he'd won the Racing Post Chase at Kempton twice – he was just the sort of horse which any yard would be proud of.

I'd ridden against him on countless occasions, but I'd never sat on him before, and when I came in for the ride in the Martell Cup round the Mildmay Course I was excited by the prospect.

Docklands Express was a lovely horse to ride. He had a similar springy feel to Remittance Man, and you could do anything with him – ask him to go long or go short, and he knew just what you meant. I found him very easy to get on with, which is just as well, as Kim Bailey's instructions to me before the race were: Whatever you do, drop him in behind and don't challenge until after the last. But I didn't get a good lead, Jamie Osborne wasn't jumping well on Arctic Call in the early stages, so I decided I just had to go on, and sent Docklands to the front. The old horse seemed to enjoy the change, and jumped very well indeed. Every time they came at him, he kept finding more, and after the last he ran on very gamely to hold off Black Humour.

Richard's own record of the race notes that Docklands Express 'enjoyed it in front', a fact conceded by trainer Kim Bailey: 'I told Richard not to hit the front until after the last, and look what happened. That's why Richard is champion jockey and I am not.'

Graham Bradley on the runner-up lodged a somewhat opti-mistic objection to Docklands Express for taking his ground after the last fence but this was overruled, and one of the most popular and durable horses in training had scored his eighteenth victory.

It was getting wetter and wetter throughout the afternoon, and by the Friday conditions were desperate.

The first was a high-class novice hurdle featuring Large Action, who had won the Tote Gold Trophy at Newbury and run a marvellous race to come third in the Champion Hurdle. He was long odds-on and my mount Cyborgo looked well beaten when Jamie Osborne took it up on Large Action three out. But then Large Action stopped in the bottomless ground and the Irish horse Monalee River came through to lead. He looked unbeatable, then when a few yards short of the winning post he too just couldn't cope any more, and Cyborgo, who is a true stayer, kept plugging on and caught him close home to win. It was one of my more unlikely victories of the season.

Thereafter the going got very bad indeed, and people began to wonder whether the Grand National could be run the next day if it became any worse. The rain just teemed down – which at least gave a good photo-opportunity to a cameraman from the *Telegraph* whose picture of me covered in mud featured on the front page on National morning!

My star ride of the meeting was Remittance Man in the Mumm Melling Chase, but like so many other horses that day he just couldn't cope with the ground. He hated the conditions and made a few jumping mistakes before fading in the home straight to finish a distant fourth behind Katabatic. That was probably the worst he's ever jumped for me, but even allowing for the ground he felt quite flat that day.

Adrian Maguire rode a double on the Friday, then, despite those fears that the meeting might have to be abandoned on account of the state of the ground, Grand National day dawned. Both Adrian and Richard had live prospects in the big race, but before that there were other winners up for grabs.

In the first I rode Her Honour, who needs much better ground and never really got into contention behind For Reg – a winner for Adrian. In the two-mile chase I was on Clay County, whom I pulled up behind Uncle Ernie. Adrian was second on Viking Flagship.

Flakey Dove ran very disappointingly in the Martell Aintree Hurdle. She'd been ridden by Mark Dwyer when she won the Champion Hurdle and I was by no means certain of getting the ride back, so when I was asked to ride her again it was a very pleasant surprise. Funnily enough, in the morning the ride on Flakey Dove at Aintree seemed much more significant than my ride in the Grand National, as I'd got the ride back against some people's expectations, and not many could see her losing. But she was well beaten, with no excuses on the day other than the ground. What was sad was that she never really looked like winning, fading early in the straight as Danoli, who at the Cheltenham Festival had won the Sun Alliance Hurdle like the Irish banker he had become, added yet more to his already massive reputation.

The Martell Aintree Hurdle was the 684th race in which Richard had ridden this season, and as he pulled the saddle off Flakey Dove and walked back into the weighing room he could reflect that, win or lose, his 685th would be one he would remember.

The next race was the Grand National.

8

FILLING THE TANK

On 9 April 1994 Richard Dunwoody weighed out for the Grand National for the tenth time.

He had first ridden in the race in 1985, at the age of twenty-one. His mount that year was West Tip, 13–2 joint favourite with Greasepaint, runner-up the previous two years. West Tip owed his prominent place in the betting to four consecutive wins culminating in the Ritz Club National Hunt Chase at Cheltenham, but in the National he tipped up at second Becher's when disputing the lead with Rupertino and the 1983 winner Corbiere. Richard's reaction that he had squandered the chance of a lifetime did not last longer than the next running, when in 1986 West Tip was an impressive winner from Young Driver.

West Tip then ran fourth in 1987 and 1988 before coming second to Little Polveir in 1989, and on all these occasions he was ridden by Richard Dunwoody.

Richard rode David Nicholson's Bigsun in 1990 (sixth behind Mr Frisk) and 1991 (pulled up at second Canal Turn after a terrible mistake at Becher's), and in 1992 Brown Windsor, who fell at first Becher's.

And then there was 1993. The bizarre chain of circumstances leading up to the running of The Race That Never Was, the Grand National declared void after a second false start had been inadequately signalled to some of the jockeys who proceeded to continue the race, has been well enough documented. But the image of Richard on Wont Be Gone Long with the broken starting tape wound around his neck – Matthew Engel in the Guardian *memorably referred to how 'Dunwoody might have been Isadora Duncan-ed' – remains one of the most potent of the whole fiasco, and it was the deeply embarrassing memory of that bungling attempt to stage a world-renowned sporting event that the 1994 running was desperate to expunge.*

As the running of the race came ever nearer, plans were unveiled to ensure that the problems would not recur. The start was repositioned to a spot which gave an unrestricted view of the run to the first fence; a loudspeaker would broadcast the starter's instructions to the jockeys; a new starting-gate mechanism would replace the antiquated structure found so sadly wanting a year earlier; and three ex-jockeys would be stationed down the track as flagmen – Advanced Flag Operators, no less – to wave down the field in the now highly unlikely event of a false start. The colour of the official recall flag was not to be revealed to the jockeys until immediately before the race in order to avoid animal rights activists staging a false recall as part of any scheme to disrupt the race, and it was this threat which clouded the run-up. Rumours were abroad that protesters were plotting to parachute onto the course to disrupt the race, and of hundreds of police officers being marshalled to thwart the activists of AAGN – Action to Abolish the Grand National.

Behind all this brouhaha was a horse race, so what of the horses?

Martin Pipe had originally entered no fewer than seventeen horses in the race, and in the event ran five. Of these, Run For Free, winner of the Welsh and Scottish Nationals in the 1992–3 season, was Mark Perrett's ride and thus did not enter Richard's calculations. Paco's Boy and Roc de Prince were both rank outsiders, so the choice which Richard faced lay between Riverside Boy, winner of the Welsh National, and the apparently rejuvenated Miinnehoma.

I couldn't take Riverside Boy on what he'd done in his previous two races. He'd been pulled up behind Just So at Chepstow when ridden by Jonothan Lower, and then pulled up in the Midlands National at Uttoxeter, ridden by Carl Llewellyn. But he liked heavy ground and was being tried in blinkers for the first time, so I was not altogether convinced that I was doing the right thing in deserting him, especially as he'd given me such a good ride in the Welsh National.

But it was very hard to get away from Miinnehoma. He was an eleven-year-old but he didn't have many miles on the clock – he'd only run in seventeen races – and his win in the 1992 Sun Alliance Chase showed that he had real class. He'd demonstrated in the past that he could go on heavy ground, had made that very encouraging comeback when beating Forest Sun at Newbury over two and a half miles, a trip much too short for him, and then he'd run well in the Cheltenham Gold Cup.

I was also encouraged by his jumping. At over sixteen hands

he's a taller horse than he might appear, but there's not much in front of the saddle, and before I rode him at Newbury I wondered how he would handle the fences there, which are probably as big as any in the country outside the National course. He jumped extremely well there and gave me a very good feel, so I was hopeful that he'd handle Aintree. But I'd never really thought of him as a National winner. I hoped he'd give me a good ride, but that was all. National day was only the third time I'd ever sat on him.

If Richard's Grand National mount was on a horse which aroused little expectation, the same could not be said of Adrian's. Moorcroft Boy, trained by David Nicholson, had thrust himself to the forefront of the Grand National picture by winning the long-distance chase at Cheltenham's New Year meeting, beating Just So by fifteen lengths, and consolidated his position as one of the leading market fancies for the Aintree race when winning the Warwick National from Chatam on the day made uncomfortably memorable for Adrian by the Ramstar incident. His pre-National race came in the Greenalls Gold Cup in late February, transferred to Kempton Park when Haydock Park was snowbound, and Moorcroft Boy ran a fine prep race to finish runner-up to Kim Bailey's Master Oats, who on the strength of that performance himself became one the leading choices for the National.

Just So, second to Moorcroft Boy at Cheltenham, was a remarkable old horse. At the age of eleven he had won just three of his thirty-three races, but needed extreme distances and, ideally, soft ground or worse to be seen to best advantage. When Just So had the conditions he needed he could be a formidable opponent for any horse, but his regular jockey

Simon Burrough knew that he had to keep after the horse relentlessly, and this landed him in hot water with the stewards at Chepstow in February, when he won the John Hughes Grand National Trial Chase over three miles five and a half furlongs in soft ground (with heavy patches). Simon Burrough picked up a ten-day suspension for his use of the whip, following an earlier four-day ban from Just So's previous race behind Moorcroft Boy. It sounded harsh, but that unceasing pressure was just what brought Just So to his best, and several shrewdies saw him as the pick of the Grand National outsiders.

As with any National, the outcome offered all sorts of intriguing possibilities for Sunday's and Monday's headlines. The Fellow, winner of the Cheltenham Gold Cup on his fourth attempt, was the latest in a distinguished sequence of contenders looking to become the only horse since Golden Miller in 1934 to win the Gold Cup and Grand National in the same year. Trained in France by François Doumen and ridden by the Polish-born jockey Adam Kondrat, he seemed to have a major chance of pulling off the historic double.

Another leading fancy was the brilliant hunter-chaser Double Silk, winner of the Foxhunters Chase at Aintree in 1993 and of eleven races in all. He was to be ridden as usual by amateur Ron Treloggen, and professional opinion was divided as to how Double Silk would cope in his first race at this level.

Much more remote in the betting but another runner which came with a built-in news story was Fiddlers Pike. The horse had good form – he was second to Riverside Boy in the Welsh National – but the story was in the identity of his jockey, 51–year-old grandmother Rosemary Henderson.

There were plenty of other familiar names in the line-up – among them Young Hustler, Elfast, 1991 Gold Cup winner Garrison Savannah, and Ebony Jane, winner of the Irish National in

1993 – and not too much attention was paid to Miinnehoma. He was easy to back in the ante-post market at around 28–1 early in National week before his odds gradually shrank to the starting price of 16–1. Moorcroft Boy started 5–1 favourite, with Double Silk 6–1 and The Fellow and Master Oats on 9–1.

But as the jockeys changed into their colours for the race, the real talking point outside on the racecourse was whether the new starting procedures would ensure a smooth send-off.

There's always great excitement all around the course on Grand National day, and a buzz in the weighing room beforehand. Just to be going out to face those fences is enough to give the preparations a real edge, and with the very heavy ground this year there was the additional thought that only a very few of us were going to get round anyway.

We get changed in two different rooms at Aintree, and before going out to the paddock this year we were all called into one room for the pre-race briefing. It is customary before the National for one of the stewards to come in and say we're not to go too fast to the first fence, but in 1994 there was extra business. We were told that the colour of the official recall flags was pink, so if we saw the pink flags waved we were to stop. Furthermore, if on the first circuit we approached a fence that was dolled off, we were to pull up and return to the start for the race to be restarted.

Then Simon Morant, who had taken over as senior Jockey Club starter on the retirement of Keith Brown last year, came in and told us that we were not to rush the tape: there were four and a half miles ahead of us, and we could afford to take it steady – at which Graham Bradley piped up from the back in a broad Yorkshire accent, 'Steady lads, long way to go!'

We were naturally aware that a great deal hung on the start

going off without hitch, but in the changing room there was no greater tension before the race than there was in any other year. As usual there was much discussion of our respective chances, and I told Simon Burrough that I really fancied his mount Just So. He'd had a fair bit of time off from the stewards following his rides on the horse, and just before we made our way to the parade ring, as he was getting his cap tied, I said to him: 'Don't take any notice of what the stewards might do – just go out and give the old horse a ride!'

In the parade ring Miinnehoma looked very well – fit and lean, a typical Martin Pipe runner. He hadn't quite come in his coat, but not many horses had by then.

The preliminaries to the National are very drawn out, but once you've got on your horse you have to treat it like any other race, and during that long walk out of the parade ring on to the course I was running through my usual pre-race routine, focusing on the race to come and concentrating on what I needed to do.

Out on the course, the thirty-six runners walked around near the start to sort ourselves into racecard order – numbers one to twenty in the circle on the left, twenty-one and above in the circle on the right. I was number eight – due to parade immediately behind the gigantic Topsham Bay, on whom I'd won the Whitbread the year before – and considered my racecard number an omen. West Tip had also been number eight before winning in 1986. In 1986, like this year, I hadn't ridden a winner at the Cheltenham Festival. And both years there had been snow on the ground when I woke up. The omens were good.

We sorted ourselves into order and paraded in front of the stands, then turned to canter down, beyond the start and over the Melling Road to take a look at the first fence. Any nerves you've been suffering leave you as you start to canter down and concentrate on the feel of your horse in its faster paces. Being quite high on the racecard, I was one of the early arrivals at the first fence. We had a good look at it and went back to the starting area, where I had my girths checked by assistant starter Gerry Scott – who himself had won the National on Merryman II in 1960. Still there was no extra tension in the jockeys because of what had happened last year – just a keenness to get on with it.

My favoured way of riding the National is to jump off handy and go down the middle. With so many loose horses around in the later stages of the race, you don't want to get too far behind, and the tactics with Miinnehoma were simple enough: get a good break, stay handy, settle him down into a rhythm. I'd told Martin that the horse had idled with me at Newbury, and that I was anxious not to get to the front too soon – though before the race this was a rather hypothetical concern!

For the Grand National it was make or break time, and although thirty fences might be waiting for the horses and jockeys setting off to tackle two long circuits at Aintree, the most daunting challenge of all was to get the start right. Within seconds all fears were allayed and the cry went up: They're off!

We were well back when we were called in, didn't all try to rush – and as a result had a great start. Although I'd aimed to break handy and then settle Miinnehoma in, he ran quite keen going down over the Melling Road towards the first, and I had to restrain him.

He jumped the first big but well, and the drop didn't affect him: he's very sure-footed, and soon learned to adapt his jumping to these unusual fences. As we went towards the second I could hear the commentary from the loudspeakers on the embankment saying some horses had fallen. I knew that there had been fallers, though I couldn't digest which they were.

A little off the lead, Miinnehoma popped over the second, then wasn't too clever at the third, the big open ditch. But his mistake was just what I needed, as it dropped him back to where I wanted to be.

He jumped the fourth OK, then at the fifth I was a little closer to the inner than was ideal. He naturally jumps to the left, so approaching Becher's Brook I let him drift to put himself right, and he was spot on, finding a very good stride and jumping neatly – though he pecked slightly.

The seventh he popped over nicely, and then it was the Canal Turn, with its ninety-degree turn to the left immediately after jumping the fence. For a horse like Miinnehoma, a left-handed jumper, the fence poses few problems, and he took it well, handily placed in fifth.

As we set off towards Valentine's Brook and the long run back towards the stands, there was a moment to take stock. Miinnehoma was going well within himself, had settled down and was relaxed and happy. I, on the other hand, was not. In the very big races the surge of adrenalin sometimes causes tension and irregular breathing, and after the Canal Turn I realized that I was too tense for my own or my horse's good. So I made a conscious effort to calm down, to say to myself that though everything was going to plan, I had to relax – keep concentrating but wind down a little. By the time we reached Valentine's I had taken a few deep breaths and was back in my own rhythm.

Miinnehoma was good at Valentine's, and here I became aware of Jamie Osborne coming through on the inner on Garrison Savannah, having a great ride. The Fellow was also nearby, and at the eleventh – two after Valentine's – out of the corner of my eye I just saw Young Hustler being knocked over by a loose horse.

Up front Ron Treloggen on Double Silk was having a marvellous ride, jumping from fence to fence. His was a spectacular performance, but I was still happy enough to sit in behind a few horses, about fifth or sixth, getting a good lead and letting Miinnehoma pop away at his fences.

Coming over the Melling Road towards the racecourse proper I saw Riverside Boy going very well in the lead, and for a moment the thought flashed through my mind that the little horse was really enjoying himself, and I might possibly have chosen the wrong one.

There seemed to be several loose horses around, and one in particular was not jumping well, so I was anxious to avoid any trouble at the two fences before the Chair. At the thirteenth – the first after the turn towards home – Double Silk fell very heavily just in front of me, and I heard a fair bit of crashing around me. Those fences have very high guard rails on the take-off side, so a horse hitting them makes a right crack.

We popped over the fourteenth and made for the Chair, the highest and narrowest jump on the course. A loose horse was in front of me, and I was thinking that the last thing I wanted was to be going into the Chair with a loose horse causing all sorts of nuisance, so I aimed to go down the inner – but Jamie on Garrison Savannah got the inside berth and I jumped the Chair one off – and to my great relief the loose horse ran out.

The Fellow put in a tremendous jump at the Chair and went past me, but by the time we came past the stands Garrison Savannah was disputing the lead with Riverside Boy, with Miinnehoma going beautifully in third.

But Riverside Boy did not fancy another circuit, and although Mark Richards managed to persuade him to go round the bend by the stables, Mark was fighting a losing battle thereafter and the horse veered right over to the far rail before refusing at the seventeenth, the first on the second circuit.

Going out into the country for the second time I called across to Jamie to ask how he was enjoying himself, but he barely had time to give an ecstatic reply before Garrison Savannah was shoved out of the race by a loose horse when just about to jump the seventeenth.

Miinnehoma had seen this loose horse trying to stop at the fence and was looking to ease himself up. With grief going on all around me I was in danger of going to the front much too soon, and my horse needed a lead to stop him backing off his fences. I was having to take a fair pull to get company, and called across to Adam Kondrat on The Fellow to give me a lead – but he too was trying not to hit the front!

Mercifully, Ebony Jane and Liam Cusack then appeared on the scene, and we had more company.

At the big ditch – the nineteenth – I was in the lead although I did not want to be, and I had to shout at Miinnehoma to get him into it. I knew that if I slacked off he'd start backing off his fences again, and to my relief Liam took it up on Ebony Jane.

It was about here that Just So and Simon Burrough appeared alongside me – about a mile earlier than I would have expected! – and I called over: 'Christ! What are you doing here?!'

Approaching second Becher's only Ebony Jane was on my outer, and I pulled Miinnehoma out far wider than he'd jumped on the first circuit. I wanted to get away from all the loose horses, who could have run down the fence and hampered him, and I wanted to minimize the effect of the drop, which despite modifications a few years back is still less marked on the outside. Things were going so well at that point that there was no point in taking unnecessary risks. He jumped the fence well enough but pecked badly on landing. For a fraction of a second I thought I might have gone: one moment his head was scraping the floor but the next he was up and galloping again. It probably looked worse than it felt, and cost him no momentum.

We put that little hiccup behind us and popped over the twenty-third upsides Ebony Jane. Everything was still going well but I was beginning to worry about the thinness of the company around us, and I also had to start wondering about Miinnehoma's stamina. He'd never gone four and a half miles before, and I felt there may be a limit.

At the Canal Turn, Liam and I were joined by Simon Burrough on Just So, and I imagined that one or two were queuing up behind to take us on. I didn't see The Fellow fall heavily, and I didn't know where Adrian was at that time. You're too busy concentrating to look round for particular horses and anyway they might disappear at the next.

At the fifth last we went through a gap in the spruce, and at the last ditch, with Just So on our inner and Ebony Jane on the outer, Miinnehoma was spot on. He was still hard on the bridle, and I had to start planning for the final stages of the race.

I went too long at the third last but the horse fiddled very well, and as we made our way back again across the Melling Road and on to the racecourse, I glanced round and there was this chestnut head with a white blaze, and the red and yellow colours – who else but Adrian on Moorcroft Boy? Even in the closing stages you have breath for essentials, and I jokingly called to him something along the lines of: 'I suppose you're going to win this one as well, you little b******!' Moorcroft Boy had been off the bridle, but when he ranged up alongside me he was going very well.

Miinnehoma was still on the bridle, Just So and Ebony Jane

were now ahead of us and Adrian was ranging up the outside. But both Ebony Jane and Just So were struggling, going nowhere, and going to the second last I didn't want to get boxed in and risk being hampered should one or both of these tired horses make a mistake or fall. So I went for a gap between them, and at the same time Adrian came round the outside.

At the second last Miinnehoma came up long for me, and all the way from that fence to the last I was letting Adrian give me a lead. My fellow was still cantering. He felt as if he'd trot up, but it was vital that he should not hit the front too soon as I was sure he'd stop, so I had to sit and suffer. Adrian started to nudge away at Moorcroft Boy – which, ironically, was not a sight I wanted to see just yet – and a loose horse, who turned out to be Young Hustler, then started to come between us.

Coming to the last, I felt I had the measure of Moorcroft Boy, even though he was just in front of me as we jumped it. Then on landing Adrian quickened away and I thought for a moment that he was going to get home after all. For about ten strides after the last he was definitely getting away from me, and all of a sudden I was off the bridle. So I pulled my whip through and gave Miinnehoma one smack, at which he started to surge forward as Moorcroft Boy came to the end of his tether. This was getting tricky! We were nearly halfway up the run-in but I couldn't put Miinnehoma under pressure as I knew he'd stop in front, so the only thing for it was to take a pull. The loose Young Hustler was still giving me a lead – but for how long?

At the elbow, halfway up the run-in, Young Hustler veered off towards the stands rail, removing my lead. I started nudging Miinnehoma, to keep him up to his work without putting the gun to his head. As I did so he spooked slightly at some traffic cones in the angle of the elbow and hesitated for a moment when the tunnel of noise hit him – as it does as you come off the elbow – and then a new threat appeared in the shape of a big black horse's head appearing on my right.

This, of course, was Just So, who was in his element in the closing stages of a four-and-a-half-mile race and had rallied after the last, cutting down Moorcroft Boy at the elbow and for a moment looking sure to go past us. He probably got to within about a neck, but the sight of him spurred Miinnehoma on. I picked up my stick and gave him a smack. He started to run on for it, and in the last hundred yards he was drawing away.

At the line he won by a length and a quarter from Just So, with Adrian and Moorcroft Boy twenty lengths further back in third and Liam Cusack and Ebony Jane twenty-five further away fourth. There were only two other finishers: Rosemary Henderson on Fiddlers Pike, whom I didn't see all the way round, and another of Martin's runners in the shape of Roc de Prince, on whom Jonothan Lower performed wonders to finish. Martin's seventeen represented a sixth of the entries, and he was responsible for a third of the finishers!

The rest of the afternoon was a bit of a blur. To say that I was ecstatic when I pulled up would be an understatement: this was the greatest thrill of my riding life, the more so as it was so unexpected. When I won on West Tip there was confidence that he would do well; with Miinnehoma we were striking out into the unknown, and I couldn't put into words how good it felt to win.

As Martin and his assistant Chester Barnes raced over to greet us, Carol came charging down from the last fence, pausing only to dance a jig with an RSPCA man.

The walk back to the unsaddling enclosure between the two police horses was bedlam as usual, though I do remember that The Duke, whose Moorcroft Boy had run a wonderful race, was one of the first to fight his way through to congratulate me, nearly being knocked over by a police horse in the process. The policeman duly received a ducal bollocking!

After unsaddling I was escorted into the weighing room by two policemen. I weighed in and gave my saddle, gloves, helmet, goggles and stick to valet Andy Townsend. (I used my old two-pound saddle that day but didn't keep it for long afterwards, as it went to a new home at the Timeform charity auction at York in June. I'd worn two pairs of goggles in the National – you pull the top pair down when they get too muddy, leaving the pair underneath clear – and they also were sold at charity events.) It was then out for the first of the television interviews, with Des Lynam for the BBC.

Miinnehoma's owner Freddie Starr couldn't be at Aintree for the race as he had to attend a rehearsal in Nottingham for a television show, but he was on the phone to Martin during the interview with Des, and I had a few brief words with him.

I then did interviews with Sky television, with BBC radio, then the official press conference (at which somebody kindly found me a glass of champagne), and watched Martin's All For Luck win the race after the National, the amateurs' chase, after which there were more interviews. Peter Bromley gave me the chart on which he had filled in all the colours for his commentary on BBC radio – as he had done in West Tip's year, and after Charter Party won the Gold Cup in 1988. They're great mementoes.

By now I was beginning to get my breath back, and the second interview which Martin and I had with Des Lynam, in the glass-fronted studio by the paddock, was a little more relaxed than the first. On the way back from there we were intercepted by a Japanese film crew for yet another interview, which ended with the question, posed via their translator: 'If Miinnehoma could speak, what would you say to him?' I couldn't think of a sensible reply.

Next stop was the box hosted by Martell, sponsors of the race, and here I met one of my boyhood idols, the legendary French jockey Yves Saint-Martin. His son Eric – who landed the 1993 Arc on Urban Sea – had won one of the races from Hong Kong which the BBC showed live early in their Grand National day transmission.

Carol was with Aidan Murphy, who had come up with us, and they fetched the trophies while I went back to the weighing room to change, and we then joined Martin for a drink in the owners' and trainers' bar.

Of all the aspects of what was for me a perfect result, one of the most important was that Martin should have trained the National winner, thereby finally burying all those sneers that he could train quantity but not quality. Miinnehoma gave him a nap hand of Nationals: the Welsh five times, the Scottish, Irish, Midlands and Liverpool.

We left the course about six, by which time it had started to rain, and took a long way home – via Warwick, where we cracked open a bottle of champagne with trainer Annabel King, Aidan's wife, and show jumper Nick Skelton, and then to the Farmhouse Restaurant at Frilford. We arrived there after ten for a meal and a party with about forty friends, and finally got home about two.

A few hours' sleep, then up at eight-thirty to drive down to Martin's for the traditional gathering to welcome the Grand National winner. Freddie Starr was there and in amazing form: I couldn't repeat much of what he said during some of his interviews – thank God most of them weren't live! The centre of attraction, Miinnehoma, was as fresh as paint after four and a half miles in that desperate going, and there wasn't a scratch on him.

We had lunch at Martin's, did the ITN news live at one,

watched a recording of the race with Freddie a couple of times, then dropped in on Carol's parents in Wantage on the way back. Breakfast television rang to ask me to go on the following morning, then we headed off to the Queen's Arms in East Garston, near Lambourn, for a bit of a party with Carl Llewellyn, Luke Harvey, and several of the other lads.

I got home about three-thirty in the morning, had a fried breakfast and a shower, and was picked up at four-thirty to be driven up to London for breakfast TV. I slept all the way up, did the show, and was driven home, where I sorted out rides for the next day, Tuesday, and had a couple of hours' sleep.

Once the collective sigh of relief at a Grand National without hitch had wafted away, Richard's ride on Miinnehoma was acknowledged to be a supreme act of jockeyship.

In the Sunday Times, *Brough Scott wrote in hushed tones:*

'The heart beats, but you have to keep your cool. It is not easy at Aintree. It is a hard place and there can only be one winner. At least this year there was a winner. There has rarely been a cooler one.

'Richard Dunwoody is still only 30 but he is an old hand. It is eight years since he won on West Tip – and it showed. With the ground heavy, this was always going to be a brutally tiring race. Miinnehoma would need all his stamina. Dunwoody had to use all the nous that has seen him through a thousand winners and might yet wrest his championship back from Adrian Maguire.'

In the Daily Telegraph *J. A. McGrath called it 'a ride at which future generations of steeplechase riders will look back and wonder: "How did he have the 'bottle' to take a pull after jumping the last fence in a National?"'*

The tabloids tended to be less interested in Miinnehoma's jockey than in his owner, and the irrepressible Freddie Starr gave them plenty of scope for headlines – 'Starr of Wonder' in the Sunday Mirror, *and numerous variations on 'Starr Turns' elsewhere, though the rider got a look in with 'Richard's A Starr' in the* News of the World.

This was show business meeting racing with a vengeance, and it was the Daily Star's *showbiz reporter, not racing correspondent, who on the Monday revealed the comedian's own explanation of Miinnehoma's name:*

'Scouser Freddie declared: "It's Gaelic for 'Lick my b****cks'."'

You learn something new every day.

The Times *reported how at the post-race party at Martin Pipe's yard Freddie Starr had waxed more lyrical when putting an arm around Richard: 'Unlike Flat jockeys – we call them bunny rabbits – these are men who ride over jumps. They break collar-bones, ribs and wrists and three weeks later they are back in the saddle.'*

But injury was mercifully low down dispatches from the 1994 Grand National. No horse was seriously injured – though Double Silk was reportedly very sore after his crashing fall – and all jockeys came back unscathed. After the humiliation of 1993, the race was back.

So was Richard's place in the sporting sun, and in the week following the National he was deluged with congratulatory cards and letters. The press had not quite done with him either, and on the Friday after the Aintree race the Daily Mirror *ran a feature which began:*

'Last Saturday he was the biggest winner in Britain. In the past week he has continued winning – the hearts of the nation.

'He was first across the line in the Grand National on Miinnehoma, and now his twinkling green Irish eyes have made Richard Dunwoody the Number One with women punters.'

Such is the price of fame.

Richard's one-line description of his ride in the record he keeps so meticulously reads: 'Always prom jumped well bar pecks Bechers held on to till went on elbow idled then ran on well whn challenged!' The exclamation mark at the end of the entry is a rare outpouring of emotion.

But perhaps the neatest description of a consummate round came from one who could appreciate its quality more than most.

Adrian Maguire had had a wonderful ride on Moorcroft Boy, and in his BBC interview with Desmond Lynam rhapsodized on the 'brilliant fun' of riding in such a race — but 'Richard was always filling the tank'.

It may have been the Grand National, but the ride on Miinnehoma still needed to be formally reported to Martin Pipe:

I wrote that he'd idled slightly in front, and my recommendation was to leave it a little later next time . . .

9

HOME STRAIGHT

After the euphoria of the Grand National victory, it was back to the daily grind on the Tuesday, and when Richard took the mount on Mariners Love in the Applied Signs Novices' Handicap Hurdle at Uttoxeter he was still fifteen winners adrift of Adrian Maguire in their relentless pursuit of the championship.

That Uttoxeter fixture was scarcely half an hour old before the gap was significantly wider, for Adrian won the first – with Richard the eight-length runner-up – and the second, before the champion pulled one back later in the afternoon on Prerogative to make the gap sixteen.

The season had less than eight weeks to run.

Carl Llewellyn and I often talked about the Grand National in the early part of the season. Carl had won on Party Politics in 1992 and I'd won on West Tip, and we always said that if we were ever to win it again we'd make sure we enjoyed ourselves properly afterwards. I think I kept to that, but eventually I had to get back to work.

The early part of the week after Aintree was quiet. One winner at Uttoxeter, Errant Knight at Worcester on the Wednesday, two rides up at Ayr on Thursday – one of which was beaten a head – then down to Taunton. No winners there, and on Saturday it was back up to Ayr for the Scottish National.

I'd never won the Scottish National, and I didn't really expect to this time on Riverside Boy. After his antics at Aintree, and remembering how he'd jinked at the bend by the stands in the Welsh National, I was wary of how he'd come round the turn by the stables at Ayr – which they have to do twice. He had a good look at the stables as we came round first time but made no attempt to run out, and on the whole he ran extremely well, disputing the lead for a long way and jumping well to finish fourth behind Earth Summit.

My best ride that day, and my only winner, was Paul Nicholls's very good novice See More Indians, who was brilliant in the big novice chase, coming right away in the straight to beat Gallateen. It was a sad race, however, as The Duke's top-class novice chaser Baydon Star, on whom I'd won at Sandown Park in February, fell with Adrian five out and later had to be put down. See More Indians himself was put down in late May after sustaining an injury while turned out in a field – a great loss, as he would have made a top-class jumper.

The week after Aintree, the task was to get back to concentrating on the title race. Robert Parsons was hard at work booking outside rides and Martin had a fair few runners, so I was still hopeful.

By the evening of Scottish Grand National day, the gap was fifteen: Maguire 170, Dunwoody 155.

During April the number of meetings starts to run down, and although there were more this year than previously, we still had the occasional day off.

The Monday after the Scottish National there was no jumping, and I drew a blank at Towcester on the Tuesday. At Cheltenham on Wednesday I had a tremendous tussle on Boscean Chieftain with Jimmy Frost and Crystal Spirit, with my fellow battling on up the hill to hold off Jimmy by one of the shortest short head verdicts I had all season.

Blank days from thirteen rides at bread-and-butter meetings at Newton Abbot, Fontwell and Taunton, but then it was Whitbread Gold Cup day at Sandown Park, one of the high-lights of the year and the only day when high-class jumping and high-class Flat racing coincide. It's a great day, but the Whitbread itself is the only jump race on the programme, and if you're chasing winners you have to make a quick getaway and head off for the evening meeting at Worcester.

In the Whitbread I rode Flashing Steel, a horse I had often gone to Ireland to school. He'd run a great race to come fourth in the Cheltenham Gold Cup and we were very hopeful. He tracked the leaders for most of the first circuit, then made a mistake at the downhill fence as the pace quickened up going away from the stands the second time. From there I was always squeezing him up down the far side. I put him under pressure going to the Pond Fence but he couldn't quicken again, and finished fifth behind Ushers Island.

As soon as I'd taken off Flashing Steel's colours it was straight into the Pipe helicopter for the flight to Worcester. Three rides there, but no winners.

Richard had had a disappointing week with just two winners,
but Adrian had scored only one. The gap was now fourteen.
By the end of the following week it was down to nine.

This was a hectic week.

On Monday I went up to Hexham – which is so far north
that Hadrian's Wall is only a few miles away – for a single
ride, Skircoat Green for Jodami's trainer Peter Beaumont. But
the long haul was well worth it when Skircoat Green won by
three-quarters of a length. I stayed overnight at West Auckland,
then went to Wetherby and won on Weaver George. Jimmy
FitzGerald, Mark Dwyer, Adrian and I then flew down to Ascot
for the evening meeting, where I won the first two on Barna Boy
and Real Progress.

On Wednesday it was off to Punchestown for the great festival
meeting. I could have ridden at Exeter that afternoon and tried to
put a few more runs on the board, but All For Luck was running
in the valuable Heineken Gold Cup at Punchestown and I was
keen to be on him. He was shaping into a very nice horse indeed,
and at the time riding him in Ireland was more important than
going to Exeter. In the event All For Luck was very disappointing,
not jumping too well and finishing eighth behind Merry Gale.

That was Wednesday afternoon. I rode Cock Cockburn for
John Queally in the 3.55 at Punchestown, then Martin, his wife
Carol and I left the course about 4.15, drove to the airstrip,
about twenty-five minutes from the course, took off about 4.45
and flew across to Staverton, near Gloucester, where I had left
my car. We drove to Cheltenham racecourse in time for me to
ride Lynch Law in the 6.35. (On the way from Punchestown to
the airport I got a call from Cathy Twiston-Davies asking if I'd
be getting to Cheltenham in time for the six o'clock, and if so
would I ride Nigel's Squire Jim in that race? David Bridgwater

had had a puncture on the way up from Exeter and wouldn't make it. The timing was impossible so I had to decline – which was a shame, as Squire Jim won with Jamie Osborne up!)

Lynch Law was beaten a short head by Fired Earth, one of the very few races all season where in a close finish I'd thought I'd won and turned out to be wrong. Matters weren't helped by the fact that Fired Earth was ridden by Adrian, who had just got back up after Lynch Law had pushed his head in front close home. There was about the width of a nostril in it – not a good omen for the championship.

My two other rides that evening – Garrison Savannah for Jenny Pitman and Billy Bathgate for Nicky Henderson – both disappointed.

The next day there was no jumping in England so it was over to Punchestown again, for one of the greatest thrills of my riding life – the La Touche Cup. This is the extraordinary race run over four miles one furlong on a course which twists and turns, using parts of the normal racecourse and various curious routes on the inside of the course, and features a wide variety of obstacles, including several grass banks (including a double bank), a couple of stone walls, a Bullfinch – that is, a very tall but loosely packed birch fence that you jump by crashing through rather than clearing – and a Becher's Brook-style fence with a drop.

I'd never ridden in the race before, so as soon as we got there I walked round part of the course with Simon McNeill, grateful that my mount Leagaune (trained by Graham McCourt's mother Mary) was not a front-runner so that I'd have to show the way! I'd ridden over similar obstacles in France so was partly prepared for the variety of jumps, and it's primarily a matter of making sure you present your horse right at each one, whatever its nature. But there are still tips to be learned. Enda Bolger, who is the best point-to-point rider in Ireland, told me to make sure that going into the double bank I was not tracking a horse which might slam on the brakes, and at the banks to take care to have my weight in the middle of the saddle, as jumping a bank is very different from jumping an orthodox chase fence, and to keep balanced in the middle of the horse's back was crucial.

Terry Casey, for whom I'd ridden a lot in the past, had schooled Leagaune and was confident about the way he'd handle himself. The horse was one of the outsiders but ran a wonderful race to come seventh behind Lovely Citizen, who had won the Foxhunter Chase at Cheltenham in 1991. In terms of pure riding thrill, this was the highlight of the season, probably more exciting than tackling the Grand National fences, and it settled an old score with my father: he was always reminding me that whatever else I may have achieved, he'd ridden in the La Touche Cup and I hadn't!

Apart from the La Touche, I had some good rides that afternoon. Magic Feeling was second to Glenstal Flagship and Thumbs Up second to 20–1 outsider Oh So Grumpy, ridden by Jamie, in the big novice chase, but Second Schedual disappointed.

Friday was back to bread and butter with four rides for Martin at Newton Abbot, where I won on Crosula, then flew up in Martin's helicopter to Bangor-on-Dee, where Strong Case won. The same evening Adrian went to Sedgefield, where he won on his first ride at the course – and it was his twenty-third birthday.

Saturday was Uttoxeter in the afternoon – one winner, Destiny Calls for Nick Gaselee – then Adrian and I flew to Plumpton, where I rode another winner.

The more the battle between us was hotting up in the final weeks of the season, the more certain parts of the press tried to manufacture needle or downright hostility between us, but it just wasn't the case. Had it been, I would hardly have had a ride to Plumpton in the helicopter hired by Colin Smith, owner of David Nicholson's yard.

I'd ridden in nine races that Saturday, thirty-four through the week at ten different fixtures, eight in Britain and two in Ireland.

With the gap down to nine – Maguire 174, Dunwoody 165 – the title race was the story keeping the jumping season in the headlines. But on Bank Holiday Monday, 2 May, it was suddenly shoved out of the way by a far more serious event.

The Swinton Hurdle at Haydock Park is the last big hurdle race of the season, and usually attracts a large field of top-class hurdlers. In 1994 there were eighteen runners, with Richard's mount Texan Tycoon vying for favouritism with Arcot, ridden by Declan Murphy.

Arcot had already made his mark on Declan Murphy's season. At Cheltenham on Mackeson Gold Cup day in November, Arcot and Murphy had taken a crashing fall, the effects of which the jockey was still feeling when partnering Bradbury Star to a heroic victory in the Mackeson itself. Murphy rode the second half of the race in blinding pain and collapsed on his way back to the weighing room.

In the Swinton Hurdle, Arcot was closing on the leader Dreams End at the last flight of hurdles. Declan Murphy asked him to stand well off but he couldn't clear the hurdle and took another crashing fall. The horse was killed, and Murphy seemed to take a severe kick in the head from the horse immediately behind, Cockney Lad, ridden by Charlie Swan.

Sport had been having a bad time, with the deaths of boxer Bradley Stone and Formula One drivers Roland Ratzenburger and Ayrton Senna only a few days previously, and the immediate diagnosis on Declan Murphy looked very grim. The Racing Post *even set up the headline 'Declan Murphy Killed in Horror Fall' in case the worst occurred. Happily, that headline was not needed: Murphy rallied in intensive care and within a few days was allowed to return home to Newmarket to continue a near-miraculous recovery. But before the end of the same week Flat jockey Steve Wood had added one more to the summer of sporting fatalities when killed after falling in a sprint at Lingfield Park.*

Both incidents left racing deeply shaken.

In the Swinton I rode Texan Tycoon for Reg Akehurst. I was told to ride handy but ended up jumping off almost in front, and in the early stages we went no gallop, unusual for a Swinton, which is usually run very fast. Down the back straight the pace picked up, and after Texan Tycoon made a mistake at the last down the far side I was soon beaten, gradually dropping out.

At the last flight I was well back, and I just saw Arcot fall in the distance. As Texan Tycoon jumped the last I could see that the horse was down, and that Declan didn't look at all good, and as I was walking the horse back after pulling up the photographer Colin Turner rushed up and said that Declan had taken a terrible fall – the worst he'd ever seen. Charlie Swan's horse just had nowhere to land and had gone right over the top onto Declan.

I had to fly off to Southwell with Martin, Chester Barnes and Charlie Swan, and on the way there we got word that Declan was critical and about to undergo an operation. There was a very sombre mood in the changing room at Southwell.

Incidents like that remind every jockey just how much we take for granted. We break legs or collar-bones and get the odd bang on the head, but these are routine injuries which you expect in this business. To think that one of us had come that close to death reminds us what could happen – but if you dwell on it you'd never go out and ride again.

In the last ten years safety has improved tremendously, and there's no doubt that the standard of the medical facilities at Haydock saved Declan's life: the paramedic team was with him in seconds and had the drip on him instantly, and that wouldn't have happened a few years ago.

Declan made an amazing recovery, but his fall made us all reflect a little.

A couple of days after the Haydock race, Richard received another anonymous piece of mail.

His correspondent had neatly snipped from the Daily Mirror *on the Tuesday morning – when Declan Murphy was still fighting for his life in hospital – Charlie Fawcus's account of the incident, headed 'MURPHY: A PERFECT GENT' and accompanied by a photograph of the moment Arcot fell. The headline had been amended by the writer to read 'DUNWOODY & EDDERY: PERFECT BASTARDS', and across the picture of Declan Murphy crashing to the ground had been scrawled the words: 'THIS SHOULD HAVE BEEN YOU. I PRAY IT WILL HAPPEN TO YOU SOON.'*

There are some very strange people out there.

I rode two winners the Monday evening at Southwell, two more the next day at Newton Abbot, and three at Uttoxeter on the Wednesday evening. Adrian also had a treble at Wetherby that evening, so the gap remained at five. The next two days were not so good, with blanks at Sedgefield (Adrian got one) and Wincanton (bad evening: two falls, one unseated, one pulled up, one fourth), but Castle Diamond won by a head at Worcester on the Saturday afternoon, and after Adrian and I had flown across to the Warwick evening meeting in Martin's helicopter I had a double: Boscean Chieftain gave me a great ride to beat Martomick a neck, and Sharp Dance won the last.

With four weeks to go, the gap was down to three, but there was no time to give the batteries a quick charge on the Sunday.

I went over to Killarney to ride Loshian for Aidan O'Brien in the big hurdle race. She ran disappointingly, but it was a great day. Killarney is a wonderfully picturesque course with the lakes and mountains in the background, and there's always a tremendous atmosphere – huge crowd, great crack, and the Taoiseach Albert Reynolds was there for a special presentation to the great commentator Michael O'Hehir, an old friend of my father. Michael O'Hehir's voice will be for ever linked with the famous pile-up at the twenty-third fence in the 1967 Grand National won by Foinavon – and Foinavon's jockey John Buckingham is now my valet on most southern tracks.

I had two rides at Towcester's Monday evening meeting. Ebony Gale was unplaced, but I got another back on Adrian, reducing the gap to two, with old General Merchant for Ron Hodges in a handicap chase. There was a slightly irritating prelude to this race. Ron had declared the horse to run in blinkers and his brother Ivor came into the weighing room to give them to me before I weighed out, and I put them on the table to show the Clerk of the Scales, who said nothing about them. Ivor took them out with the saddle and put them on the horse, then while he was going round the paddock the stipendiary steward came up and said that General Merchant had not been declared to wear blinkers. It wasn't in the racecard, wasn't in the racing papers, and they couldn't check with Weatherbys — where declarations are made — as the office would be closed.

So we had to take them off. In the event it didn't make too much difference to the old horse, who at the age of fourteen knows all about the game, and he still won well enough without them. But a couple of days later we discovered that it had been an error at Weatherbys. If it had been a trainer in the wrong there would have been fines imposed, but someone in the bureaucracy should also be held responsible. Had General Merchant run in blinkers and no-one noticed that he was not declared for them, he could have been disqualified.

I had two winners, both for Martin, at Chepstow the next day. Pridwell won the novices' hurdle at 3–1 on to bring me within one winner of Adrian, and that was still the position when we went out for the last race on the card, a National Hunt Flat race. At the start I said to Adrian (though I'm not entirely sure I meant it): 'If I win this, we'll stop for the season,' but he didn't reply . . .

Distant Echo duly won the bumper, which was particularly pleasing as he's owned by Mel Fordham, racecourse photographer and Carol's boss. Until recently most bumper races in this country were restricted to conditional jockeys, but it's a good idea that they've been opened up, because a large field of inexperienced riders on inexperienced horses is not the ideal recipe for teaching either. Conditionals learn more from riding with their seniors, and it's much better for the horses.

That double brought Richard level with Adrian for the first time since the first day of the season way back in July, but the bookmakers were in little doubt now about the destination of the title: Hill's now went 5–2 on Dunwoody, 7–4 Maguire.

Despite the betting, the stage was set for a dramatic final few

days of a long and arduous season, and the next day saw the
action rapidly moving between three locations as both jockeys
rode at three separate meetings. It was the first time either of
them had gone to such lengths in search of winners, and for
Richard a day spent rushing between Hereford, Southwell and
Huntingdon brought him eight riding fees but no winners.

Adrian had nine rides and regained the title lead when winning
on the first of them, Formal Affair in the opener at Hereford.
He was not to know it, but it would be nearly two weeks, and
forty-nine rides, before he rode another.

We both went up to Perth: I had three rides – one third, and
the other two both pulled up! The following day – Friday the
Thirteenth – I went down to Martin's to school in the morning
and rode four at Newton Abbot in the evening, winning on
Errant Knight to get back level again.

The following morning I was up as usual at six-thirty for a
quick cup of coffee but this time no toast, then an hour in the
bath to get my body weight down to nine-ten, as I was riding
Merlins Wish at Bangor at ten stone.

At different stages of the season, with all its ups and downs,
the issue of 'pressure' had come up time and time again. Was
there pressure on Richard before a particular ride in a big race,
or pressure as his title seemed to be slipping away? As he fought
back, was there the additional pressure of possibly getting close
but still losing?

For psychologist Peter Terry, 'the key element of pressure is the
doubt in the mind of sportsmen that they are capable of meeting
the challenge they've set themselves. That doubt causes anxiety,
which sets off a chain reaction and deflects your thoughts from
the outcome to the process.'

*For Richard, as he came to the verge of taking the lead he had
so desperately craved, outcome was all.*

That Saturday at Bangor-on-Dee illustrated how pressure is
related to expectation. I thought I'd get the title lead by winning
the first on On The Sauce, but he was second. I thought I'd
win the second on Flintlock for Nicky Henderson – and he
too got beaten. At this point I began to become a little uptight,
because the day was not living up to my – or other people's –
expectations.

But all was well with my third ride, Merlins Wish, who took
it up two out and stayed on well to beat Noblely by four lengths
– my 180th winner of the season. Adrian had six rides that day
but was stuck on 179.

It was wonderful to have taken the lead after such a long
slog to get there, but I'd experienced a similar situation from
the other side in the past when I was twenty clear of Scu after
he'd broken his leg, and he caught me. That year there was no
pressure on me, as everyone assumed that he'd get the lead back,
and as he was riding for Martin there was an inevitability about
the situation.

*The race to the wire for the jockeys' title was drawing far more
media attention to the dying embers of the jumping season than
was usual, with racing writers having to balance coverage of the
Derby and Oaks trials with close attention to the duel. The day
after Richard had taken the lead at Bangor on 14 May, Brough
Scott in the* Sunday Times *looked forward to the remaining three
weeks of the season:*

*'It won't get any easier. The weather may be balmy, but
the ground gets harder and the form of conveyance decidedly
worse. The top horses are already on their summer break. This*

week's nags are those unable to compete at the high time of the season. This is their chance of fulfilment. Not all are that keen on taking it.'

With Richard one up, William Hill cut his odds to 4–1 on, Adrian 11–4.

Taking the lead was one thing, but keeping it meant there was a great deal of work still to do. I'd had a good season as far as injury was concerned, never having missed a ride – let alone a day – through the effects of a fall, whereas Adrian was suffering the odd knock. But in jump racing anything can happen to interfere with your plans – the Raggerty race at Nottingham was evidence enough of that – and I was just hoping that we could both stay in one piece until the very end of the season.

From the point of view of self-preservation I'd had a very good season, but I was well aware that the final period, when the ground is hard and some of the horses of lesser ability, is a dangerous time.

When I was at school a master named Mr Hemery used to say that if you go into a rugby tackle in a half-hearted way, that's when you get hurt, and I've always tried to apply the same idea to riding over jumps. If you're only giving your horse half a ride, if you're backing off, that's when you are going to fall and get injured. On an untried novice hurdler somewhere like Taunton on firm ground you may experience a little anxiety, but you have to control it, and concentrate on your stride and on your race tactics. If you're not positive about everything in a race then the horse is going to start making mistakes that may have been avoided.

On the Monday the duel recommenced.

Adrian hadn't had a winner since Hereford, but with three weeks to go it was vital to maintain my concentration.

On my way to Fontwell on the Monday I went again to Peter Terry, and he stressed that I was to prepare myself mentally for Adrian having a good run and maybe getting ahead of me again. If so, I was not to let this affect me, but keep focusing on my own performance. If I was riding against Adrian, I was not to let his involvement influence my own tactics, not wonder where he was in the race. All common sense, really, but something you have to be reminded of. There had been times, as the season wore on and the championship became more tense, that I'd found myself being over-influenced by Adrian's presence in a race, and Peter Terry's message for the last phase of the season was simply to keep my head down and get on with riding each race as best I could.

One winner at Fontwell – Celcius beating Adrian on Bondaid – took Richard's lead to two. Tuesday there was no jump racing, Wednesday no winners from four rides at Worcester. On Thursday Mine's An Ace won at Exeter, but the same day brought disappointment with Skipping Tim, a wonderful old servant to Richard and to Martin Pipe, who was tailed off behind Naughty Nicky in the claiming chase and at the age of fifteen faced retirement.

Two more winners at Stratford on Friday evening, then another double the following evening at Warwick, and with two weeks of the season to go Richard had stretched his lead to seven. Adrian had not ridden a winner for ten days, and the bookmakers were no longer taking bets.

Into the penultimate week of the season. Castle Blue took Richard's lead to eight at Market Rasen on the Monday. At the same meeting Adrian bruised his elbow when unseated in the fourth race and gave up his final two rides. But in the first race at Sedgefield on the Tuesday afternoon he finally brought his losing run to an end by winning on Buckra Mellisuga, his first winner in forty-nine rides. Three races later Richard hit back with Saraville to put the gap back to eight, and the prospect of either jockey – or both – reaching 200 winners in the season, a feat previously achieved only by Peter Scudamore in 1988–9, became ever more real. Whether or not the magic figure would be reached, with Adrian back in the winning mould the title race would go to the wire.

On Wednesday 25 May, with just nine racing days to go to the end of the season on 4 June and Richard those eight winners clear, came an unexpected setback. It was revealed that All For Luck had tested positive to a banned substance when winning the March Novices' Handicap Chase at Newbury on 26 March, and was certain to lose the race. The Jockey Club declared itself 'satisfied that no malpractice was intended', but under the rules All For Luck would inevitably be disqualified when the case came up at the end of June.

By then, of course, the season would be over, so the position threw statisticians into a quandary. Should one winner be deducted from Richard's running total in anticipation of that disqualification, or would the title be decided only on the results as they stood formally at the end of racing at Market Rasen on the final day?

For some weeks both the trade papers had been running graphically displayed daily bulletins on the duel – current score, plus rides for the day ahead, and the Racing Post, *whose statistics were to be considered official for purposes of adjudicating the championship, soon removed one winner in expectation of the disqualification, while the* Sporting Life *for the time being kept to the scores as posted.*

At the time all this discussion seemed academic, as the idea that by the evening of 4 June the gap might have shrunk to the point where one winner could make the difference seemed, to say the least, improbable.

Richard himself could afford to be philosophical, pointing out that he had gained a winner – My Cup Of Tea at Newton Abbot in September – from a disqualification earlier in the season. Swings and roundabouts.

On the Wednesday at Cartmel, the day the All For Luck problem was revealed, Richard picked up a spare ride from Adrian, who despite having ridden the previous day thought it wise to give his injured shoulder more time to heal. The spare – Potato Man – ran third, but there was another Dunwoody double with Love You Madly and Windward Ariom.

That was Richard's last winner of the week. Adrian pulled another back when winning on Formal Affair at Hereford on the Thursday to reduce the gap slightly. Richard could not afford to ease up.

On the Friday evening I went to Towcester for three rides. I was not confident about any of them, though old Henry Mann, who had fallen at the first in the Grand National when ridden by Charlie Swan, would have been far too good for his modest opponents in the three-mile-one-furlong handicap chase if he had been at anything like his best form: he'd won the Coral Golden Hurdle Final at Cheltenham back in 1990, though by now he was getting a bit long in the tooth at the age of eleven, and he'd not won a race for over two years.

He'd always been quite hard work to ride, and pulling out of the bottom towards the home straight I was chasing him along in a vain attempt to keep in touch. In the straight he actually started to run on a bit alongside another horse, and going to the last I thought he might get fourth. He then kept on at one pace to finish sixth, but as soon as he'd crossed the line and pulled up he got the staggers. I steered him towards the wing of the fence just beyond the stands and got off. He was battling to stay on his feet but finally the lights just went out and down he went. His owner Lynn Wilson thought the world of him. He was a smashing old horse, and it was a very sad moment.

I also rode General Merchant. He took it up two out, but this time he stopped, even with the blinkers, once he'd jumped the last and was caught close home by Young Alfie, ridden by Adrian, who also won that evening on Res Ipsa Loquitur.

Ignoring the probable loss of the All For Luck race, this narrowed the gap to seven – Richard 190, Adrian 183.

During those last few days when the gap was getting so close again, I wasn't getting too worried about how Adrian was doing – though I have to admit that on the Saturday when I was at Cartmel and he was at Hexham I sneaked the odd look at the results in the on-course mobile betting shop.

He cannot have been pleased by what he saw. Adrian had pulled another back with Seon while Richard himself had drawn another blank: 190 to 184 – or, if you included the All For Luck loss to crank up the excitement, 189 to 184.

The duellists lunched together on Sunday, along with fellow jockeys Carl Llewellyn, Brendan Powell and Luke Harvey, then drew a deep breath and got stuck into the final week. And like a boxer touching gloves with his opponent before fighting out the last round, Robert Parsons phoned Dave Roberts on the Monday morning to wish him all the best. The seconds, like the duellists themselves, were polite to the end.

On the Monday morning I went over to Nicky Henderson's to school Tudor Fable over fences. He was due to run at Worcester the following day, and we wanted to give his confidence that little extra boost.

From Nicky's I flew up to Cartmel, where I won the first on Commanche Creek. After getting tailed off on Sovereign Niche it was a mad dash to get down to Uttoxeter, arriving with about three minutes to spare. Three rides there yielded a fall off Safari Park and two well beaten, and meanwhile Adrian had had a double at Huntingdon. Deducting one for All For Luck, the gap was just four.

I had six rides the next day at Worcester and got one winner back with Highly Reputable (with Adrian second on Gladys Emmanuel), though my other rides that day disappointed – including Tudor Fable, who was second when odds-on favourite.

Lots of horses finished lame on the firm going at Worcester that day, including five of the nine runners in the handicap hurdle. The course will have to do a better job with the ground when they start midsummer racing there in 1995.

Adrian had flown up to Hexham's evening meeting for rides in some of the earlier races, and by the time I got up there he'd pulled one more back with Down The Road. But fourteen-year-old Clever Folly gave me a wonderful ride to win the fifth from Strong Approach, with Adrian in third on Seon. Walter Bentley, Seon's trainer, had threatened to run him twice that day if it meant giving Adrian an extra opportunity for a winner, but mercifully he thought better of the idea!

I came third on Station Express in the last, then flew down to the airport at Kidlington, near Oxford. Ronnie Beggan was in the plane, over the moon from riding at Hexham that evening to give him a full house of wins on all British jumps tracks. He'd won on his last ever ride, Kinda Groovy in the last, and flying back he was absolutely delighted. All of us, Ronnie included, found it unbelievable that anyone could get on such a high by riding the winner of the last race at a Hexham evening meeting!

I got home about one-thirty, and luckily there was no jumping the next day.

But the next day there was the Ever Ready Derby at Epsom, accentuating how the final moments of the jumps season are enmeshed with the big days on the Flat.

I like the big Flat occasions and I'd thought of going to the Derby, but instead went to Val Ridgeway to have some physiotherapy, following my fall on the Monday. I ended up watching the Derby quietly at the Queen's Arms with a couple of the lads.

It seemed to be generally agreed that for the purposes of the title we should knock off the All For Luck race – we had, after all, added on the My Cup Of Tea in my favour – so come Thursday morning I thought of myself as five clear.

I picked up a couple of spares for Nigel Twiston-Davies at Uttoxeter that day, and the first of these, Ghia Gneuiagh, won very easily. That was my only winner of the day, but Adrian rode three – Special Account, Comedy Road and Otter Bush – to cut the gap right back to three, with two days to go.

This was getting too close for comfort, and on the Friday morning I went to see Peter Terry for a booster jab of psychology. Peter stressed, as he had so often through the season, that the task was to keep thinking positively, keep my mind on the job, and – this was one of his key phrases – control the controllable. Don't worry about what you can't control – about whether Adrian is riding another winner. Concentrate on what you can control – riding another winner yourself.

On Friday evening we were at Stratford. The weather was not too clement, but there was an enthusiastic crowd and at the very least the championship race was maintaining interest in the jumps season right up to the end, whereas normally it flags soon after the National, and all but dies completely following the Whitbread.

There had been a tremendous increase in media attention, and although it was a tiny bit monotonous having to say the same thing over and over to so many interviewers – no, Adrian and I do not hate each other, yes, we'll keep going right to the end – we knew that this was all good publicity for the sport.

At Stratford, Adrian won the first on Southampton, and I was third on Sophism. The gap was two. He was second in the second and I pulled up. Gap still two. In the morning papers Adrian was not down for a ride in the third, but Dean Gallagher, due to ride Res Ipsa Loquitur (on whom Adrian had won a week earlier), broke down on the way to the races and arrived at the course too late to take the ride. Adrian came in for a useful-looking spare – even more useful-looking after he'd won by six lengths. The gap was down to one.

After that race, in which I was unplaced on Merlins Wish, I went into the changing room sauna for half an hour. I needed to do ten stone on Take A Flyer for Ron Hodges in the last, and I couldn't leave anything to chance. I got rid of a pound and a half, then picked a spare on Howgill for Reg Hollinshead (started favourite but finished fourth).

Take A Flyer duly did his bit, winning by three lengths from Forgetful: I was a little bit hard on him, and must have posed the stewards a bit of a borderline case! Going into the final day I was again two up.

The duel was nearly over.

10

THE FINAL DAY

The last occasion on which the jump jockeys' championship remained undecided until the final day of the season was in 1971, when Graham Thorner clinched it at the Market Rasen evening meeting to beat Terry Biddlecombe by seventy-four winners to seventy-two.

The climax to the 1993–4 season was different in several ways. Not only had the protagonists amassed totals unheard of two decades ago – Adrian Maguire's seventy-fourth winner, for example, was Spikey at Ascot on 19 November – but the duel had captured the imagination of the racing public as no other jockeys' title had. Much of this was to do with the personalities and respective positions of the duellists – ace-cool ultra-professional champion, wonder kid – and the built-in drama of their head-to-head battle had been fuelled by events throughout the season. Both had had great highs and great lows. Now it was time to decide who was the victor.

There were additional matters on racing's mind on Saturday 4 June, notably the 216th running of the Oaks at Epsom, where the big talking point was whether Bulaxie could justify favouritism, or whether Balanchine would gain compensation for her wafer-thin defeat in the One Thousand Guineas.

Jumping's two meetings were in the afternoon at Stratford, where the first race was at 2.50 and the last at 5.55, and in the evening at the small Lincolnshire town of Market Rasen, with its opener at 6.25 and final race at 9.05.

Blessed as they both were, neither jockey could be in two places at once, and prognoses of how the title race might end hinged on whether each seemed to have the stronger overall book of rides.

I looked to have a better Stratford than Adrian, with four runners for Martin, three of whom were forecast to start favourite, and Armashocker for Bob Jones in the last. The idea was to fly to Market Rasen in time to get there for the third and have rides in the last four.

Adrian had a stronger-looking set of rides at Market Rasen than I did, and he planned to get up there before me, after riding in just two races at Stratford.

Errant Knight, my first at Stratford, looked a certainty – he started at 3–1 on – and ran like one. Adrian's ride in that race, Space Fair, cocked his jaw at the fourth from home just as I moved upsides him and ran out, leaving Errant Knight to saunter home twenty-five lengths clear of old Nos Na Gaiothe.

I was three clear of Adrian. So far so good.

He did better than I in the next race, coming fourth on Bootscraper while I pulled up on Celcius, then he took off for Market Rasen in a helicopter.

The third at Stratford was the Horse and Hound Cup, a big hunter chase, and after that I was back in action.

Lynch Law was favourite for the two-and-three-quarter-mile hurdle but by no means certain to beat Jim Old's Wick Pound. I let Wick Pound give me a lead over the last two, then asked Lynch Law to quicken, which he did without fuss to go on and win by eight lengths.

Four clear, but still I couldn't relax.

Saraville in the three-mile handicap chase was the third favourite I'd ridden that afternoon, and she didn't let me down, staying on well under pressure despite a mistake two out to win by seven lengths from Prudent Peggy.

Armashocker couldn't sew everything up in the last, and as I made for Martin's helicopter for the flight to Market Rasen I was five clear with six races to go. I was even beginning to feel hopeful.

Meanwhile Market Rasen was clearly enjoying its day in the limelight. One of the neatest and best-run of the small jumping tracks, and proof that atmosphere comes from people out to enjoy themselves and not just from quaint old buildings, it rarely steals the headlines in the sporting press.

But tonight was different, and a crowd of around 7,000, at least 1,000 greater than usual at this end-of-term evening meeting, thronged the enclosures. On the lawn in front of the stands the Market Rasen (Rhoades Saddlery) Band oom-pahed their way through an extensive repertoire. Did they have a couple of Saw Doctors numbers up their sleeves in the event of a Dunwoody victory to celebrate? The weather could not quite make up its mind whether to join in the fun or not, alternately threatening rain and then bathing the course in sunshine.

Early arrivals at the course at five o'clock, over an hour before the first race, might have been intrigued to see many racegoers in the stands and car parks training their binoculars on the infield. But follow their line of sight and the target of their curiosity was apparent – a dark green helicopter. As the rotor blades slowly whirred to a halt a figure carrying a hold-all emerged, and a buzz went around: 'It's Maguire!'

It was indeed Maguire, but as he arrived Dunwoody was scoring his second win at Stratford, and half an hour later racegoers crowded into the bars to watch the television screens as Saraville effectively put the championship out of Adrian's reach.

Those hoping for a truly sensational finish, one which went down to the very last race, were disappointed. Dunwoody was five up and there were six races to go. Maguire couldn't possibly win now.

Or could he?

In the first race he rode 6–4 favourite Wayward Wind, who took the lead going to the third last and never looked in danger thereafter. The gap was back to four, with five races to go.

In the second, a selling hurdle, Adrian rode another favourite, a horse with the highly appropriate name of It's Unbelievable: he was trained like Adrian's first winner of the evening by John White, who had done so much to support Adrian at the beginning of the season and give him the flying start on which his championship bid had been founded.

It's Unbelievable lived up to his name, reducing the gap to three with an emphatic win over Coeur Battant. One racegoer, not entering into the spirit of the evening at all, was heard to pronounce: 'I'm fed up with Adrian Maguire.'

▼

After Saraville won at Stratford I was happy enough, but I still wouldn't let myself believe that I'd won. The season had had so many ups and downs that nothing would have surprised me. I thought Adrian would win the first three at Market Rasen, and after that, who knew what might happen?

As It's Unbelievable was being led round the unsaddling enclosure for the post-selling race auction, the sound of the auctioneer's voice momentarily had to contend with the sound of another helicopter landing, and the word spread around: 'He's arrived.'

The first two at Market Rasen took place as we were in the air on the way over from Stratford. For both races, Robert Parsons (who was at home in Kettering) called up one of the commentary lines and phoned me in the helicopter on his other phone, relaying to me what was happening – so I knew that Adrian had won the first two.

The third would be crucial. Adrian was on the 6–4 favourite Bobby Socks for Richard Lee. I rode Lapiaffe and led for much of the way, but going down the back straight Martin Brennan on Call Me Early took it up. Adrian followed Martin through and appeared to be going very easily, and as I went to the last I thought that Bobby Socks would probably win: my mind wasn't focusing on my stride so much as his! The two leaders were in the air together and from about fifteen lengths behind them it wasn't easy for me to see which was ahead, but just after they passed the post I could tell that Martin had crossed over in front of Adrian – and that was the moment I knew that I couldn't be beaten for the championship.

I still had to make sure I was the outright winner, and there were other horses to be ridden. Rapid Mover in the fourth finished seventh, just one place behind Adrian on Logical Fun, and the title was assured.

That was it – all over!

Rapid Mover may have been well beaten, but as he came up the straight at Market Rasen the elements provided Richard with a triumphal arch in the form of a huge double rainbow painted across the evening sky, one end somewhere beyond the back straight, the other in the unsaddling enclosure.

The band – perhaps coincidentally, perhaps not – played the Abba song about how the winner takes it all, and as Richard brought Rapid Mover in to unsaddle, a small child, no doubt making sure that his memory of an historic evening would be accurate, asked: 'Which one is Dunwoody, Dad?'

Castle Cross was tailed off in the two-and-a-half-mile novice chase – Adrian came second on Bondaid – and then it was time for the presentations.

Sponsorship of the championship by William Hill had done a lot to focus attention on the title, and Hill's made a presentation to the top conditional jockey Tony Dobbin, to Adrian as runner-up in the jockeys' championship, and to myself, then some of the other jockeys lifted us both on to their shoulders for the photos. There was just time for a few quick press interviews. My main theme was 'I'm not going through all that again', and Adrian told them that Dave Roberts had already booked him three rides for Bangor-on-Dee on the first day of next season!

I had to break away from the throng and then run the gauntlet of autograph hunters on the way to the paddock for my last ride of the season, Pridwell in the 'Season's Over' Novices' Hurdle. Martin had been planning to run him in the race for some weeks and we expected him to go well, but possibly he didn't get the trip of two miles, five and a half furlongs, as he faded early in the straight to finish seventh. Adrian was third on Super Coin.

We got through a bottle of champagne in the weighing room while getting changed, and I had more television and radio interviews to do. I didn't leave the course until about ten, then continued the celebrations in Newark with Mark Low (who had come on the skiing trip) and Graham Bradley.

The day after the season had ended so dramatically at Market Rasen, Richard joined several of his fellow jockeys at the wedding of Brendan Powell. Adrian was best man.

A busy couple of months lay ahead, with a holiday in Barbados, a trip to Ireland for the Irish Derby and the chance to join Irish friends in cheering on Jackie Charlton's team in the World Cup, riding in Ireland and Jersey, and the investiture at Buckingham Palace on 20 July when he would receive his MBE.

First, however, a more mundane pleasure.

On the Monday after Market Rasen I drove into Swindon, went to a McDonald's and sat there reading the paper with a cheeseburger and a chocolate milk shake. I don't think I've ever enjoyed a drink more.

11

EASING UP

As Richard sat savouring his Swindon cheeseburger, the racing world bathed in the afterglow of a memorable battle.

For Alan Lee in The Times, *'This is a story that has done more than sustain rabid jumping fans. It has presented racing in a new light to those with jaundiced images of the filthy rich and filthy betting shops. It is a tale of real people and, fittingly, it climaxed on the day that the Oaks, like the Derby, was Arab preserve.' (The Oaks had been won by Balanchine, owned by the Maktoum brothers' Godolphin Racing and trained in Dubai.)*

In his column in the Racing Post, *Paul Haigh wrote of 'what may have been the greatest, longest-running battle in the history of British race-riding', before tackling the question of which is the better jockey. He weighed the qualities of each rider before concluding:*

'Maguire. It's got to be Maguire. By a head, or even a neck –
and by more than that too, maybe, if neither of them was messed
about by any stewards and any namby-pamby whip rules.

'But then again. Think of Dunwoody, so cool and calm and
determined. Think of Miinnehoma. Think of . . .

'Ahh, forget it. Evens the field for next year?

'And may the best man win.'

Evens the field for next year? As good as. William Hill went
5–4 on Richard, evens Adrian, and Richard's Market Rasen vow
against going through all that again was not long odds-on to sur-
vive a few weeks' relaxation, a point picked up by Richard's friend
and riding colleague Marcus Armytage in the Daily Telegraph:

'It will probably be a couple of days before either winds down
enough to feel tired. The thing about Dunwoody, though, is that
he doesn't like being second and statements made before the
smoke has cleared from the battlefield are always going to be
open to change when the adrenalin flows again.'

Marcus Armytage also pointed out that Adrian's mounts had
won £90,000 more than Richard's, illustrating that while the Pipe
connection may have meant winners, the job as David Nicholson's
jockey was a stronger guarantee of big earnings. Win and place
money earned by Richard was £1,098,719; by Adrian, £1,193,917.
(Nicholson himself was champion trainer for the first time, with
prize money of £754,069, after five consecutive years of Martin Pipe
ruling the roost. Martin was runner-up with £719,607.)

Richard's official total of winners at the end of the final day
– without the All For Luck deduction – was 198 winners to
Adrian's 194; Jamie Osborne was third with 105, Norman
Williamson fourth with 104. Richard had missed the magic 200
mark by a whisker, but his total none the less represented the
second highest ever notched up by the top jump jockey, beaten
only by Peter Scudamore's phenomenal 221 in 1988–9.

Those 198 winners came from 891 rides, a strike rate of 22 per cent. Adrian's 194 from 915 represented a strike rate of 21 per cent, and there was similarly just one percentage point between their wins-to-runs ratios for their main trainers. Martin Pipe provided Richard with 314 rides, of which 94 won: 30 per cent. David Nicholson gave Adrian 213 rides of which 61 won: 29 per cent. But 47 per cent of all Richard's winners were for Pipe, just 31 per cent of Adrian's for The Duke, which illustrates the significant role played in the Maguire bid by outside rides.

Second in the list of trainers providing winners for Richard was Ron Hodges with thirteen, followed by Nicky Henderson (ten), Charlie Mann (nine), Bill Turner (seven) and David Nicholson (six): what a difference The Duke's half dozen made!

Adrian's highly influential second trainer was John White with thirty-five winners, of which seventeen were on the board by the end of September and twenty-two notched up by the turn of the year, illustrating the important part played by White as Adrian built up his lead.

Both jockeys exceeded the previous record number of rides during a season, both Adrian's 915 and Richard's 891 beating Richard's 740 in 1992–3.

Understandably, Adrian's total of 194 winners represents the highest ever by a loser in the jump jockeys' race, and his prize money accrued also set a fresh record, £1,193,917 beating Richard's 1992–3 total of £1,101,876.

During the season Richard rode at thirty-eight of Britain's forty-three jumping tracks – the exceptions were Carlisle, Catterick, Doncaster, Kelso and Newcastle – and overseas at Belmont Park and Camden in the USA and at Fairyhouse, Killarney, Leopardstown (where Chirkpar was his only overseas winner), Listowel, Punchestown and Tralee in Ireland.

In Britain he won races on 131 different horses, and had particular cause to be grateful to Martin Pipe's Errant Knight, who provided him with five victories, all between 13 April and 4 June. The two other horses he rode to victory five times were Martin Pipe's Pridwell (who gave him two of his eleven victories on all-weather surfaces) and Charlie Mann's Sheer Ability. But had you staked a pound on every Dunwoody runner you would have ended up owing your bookmaker £91.10.

Richard was runner-up 145 times, third in 117 races, had thirty-nine falls and was unseated eight times (though he did not miss a single ride through injury); he had one run-out and pulled up in sixty races; 290 of his rides started favourite, of which 117 won.

Two other telling statistics from Richard Dunwoody's 1993–4 season concern his agent Robert Parsons. Without recourse to a sauna, Robert lost half a stone during the first half of the year, and his telephone bill for the quarter covering the last period of the duel shows that he made 2,751 calls. Robert had been one of the vital seconds in the Dunwoody corner, as had sports psychologist Peter Terry, who regularly brought Richard a sense of perspective and focus when he most needed it. But the man who had provided the most direct input to the championship victory was Martin Pipe:

The support I received from Martin during the final weeks of the season was fantastic, and I was especially grateful that he supplied the three winners at Stratford on the final day – Errant Knight, Lynch Law and Saraville – to clinch the title.

Before I moved to Martin there had been murmurings that going there would turn out the worst decision of my career, and the whispers grew louder and louder – and more public – at some stages of the season. But we proved the critics wrong, and the fact that Martin provided nearly half my winners speaks for itself.

*And a final Dunwoody verdict – for the time being at least – on
Adrian Maguire, close friend and arch rival:*

Adrian is above all a natural rider, probably the most natural I've
ever ridden against. He has a real rapport with every horse he rides,
and that priceless ability to see a stride. Horses run for him, and he
can continue to get the best out of them from a long rein – not a style
it is easy to emulate, but one which makes horses feel comfortable.

It is so early in his career that comparisons with other great
jockeys I've competed against are dangerous, but Adrian does
seem to combine the qualities of horsemanship and jockeyship
in a way which I have not previously seen.

John Francome was a great horseman, though had to work at
being a jockey, especially – in his early days' riding under Rules
– in a finish. Scu was a more natural jockey but perhaps less of
a horseman. Adrian is both to an unbelievable degree, and with
jockeys like him in action over the next few years jumping will
become more competitive and jockeyship more professional.

*Adrian looked a pretty fair bet to become champion jump jockey
in the fullness of time, but at the close of the 1993–4 season the
champion was still Richard Dunwoody.*

The end of the season was for me like the valve being released on
a pressure cooker, and with the luxury of hindsight it was possible
to appreciate what a marvellous duel it had been.

It had been extraordinarily exhausting, mentally much more than
physically. I was physically drained from wasting over the last two
days of the season, but mentally I was wired to the moon.

I meant what I'd said at Market Rasen on the last evening of the
season: I won't be going through all that again.

Or will I?

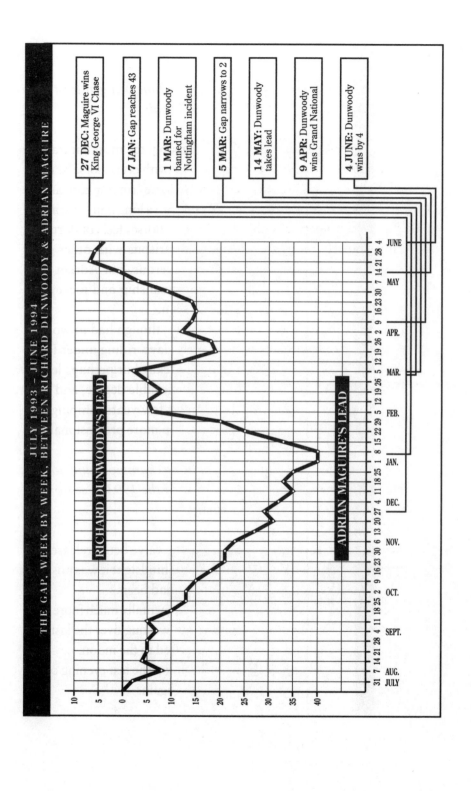

THE GAP, WEEK BY WEEK, BETWEEN RICHARD DUNWOODY & ADRIAN MAGUIRE

JULY 1993 – JUNE 1994

27 DEC: Maguire wins King George VI Chase

7 JAN: Gap reaches 43

1 MAR: Dunwoody banned for Nottingham incident

5 MAR: Gap narrows to 2

14 MAY: Dunwoody takes lead

9 APR: Dunwoody wins Grand National

4 JUNE: Dunwoody wins by 4

RICHARD DUNWOODY'S LEAD

ADRIAN MAGUIRE'S LEAD

1993 – 94 SEASON: TOP TEN JOCKEYS

WINS-RIDES		JOCKEY AND LOWEST RIDING WEIGHT SINCE JAN 93	TRAINER GIVING MOST WINNERS	ALL RIDES WINS-RIDES		2ND	3RD	£1 STAKE	WIN & PLACE £ PRIZE MONEY	NH FLAT & HURDLES WINS-RIDES	CHASES WINS-RIDES	FAVOURITES WINS-RIDES
198-891	22%	R Dunwoody 10-0	M C Pipe	94-314	30%	145	117	-91.10	1,098,719	113-546	85-345	117-290
194-915	21%	A Maguire 9-9	D Nicholson	61-213	29%	175	112	-83.51	1,193,917	108-556	86-359	97-276
105-497	21%	J Osborne 10-0	O Sherwood	28-115	24%	75	54	-51.50	703,834	64-293	41-204	57-139
104-582	18%	N Williamson 9-6	K C Bailey	67-244	27%	103	65	-120.81	538,856	35-320	69-262	46-123
89-409	22%	P Niven 10-2	Mrs M Reveley	75-257	29%	70	45	-80.11	455,939	52-256	37-153	54-140
68-556	12%	M A Fitzgerald 10-0	N J Henderson	20-130	15%	53	73	-151.90	336,462	31-327	37-229	25-74
65-397	16%	G McCourt 10-4	N Tinkler	14-83	17%	58	49	-66.83	297,654	46-256	19-141	29-75
58-371	16%	D Murphy 10-0	J T Gifford	30-184	16%	52	51	-64.60	455,315	32-225	26-146	27-70
58-398	15%	D Bridgwater 10-0	N A Twiston-Davies	34-135	25%	38	41	-17.69	333,984	29-254	29-144	21-50
48-265	18%	L Wyer 10-0	M H Easterby	26-96	27%	36	42	+31.87	231,914	30-182	18-63	25-61

© Racing Post